Published December 2018
© Copyright 2018 Julie Norton
Branchwood Publishing
www.branchwoodpublishing.co.uk

All rights reserved. This book may not be reproduced in any form, in whole or in part, without written permission from the editor.

The Reservist

by John Walter (Wally) Harmer

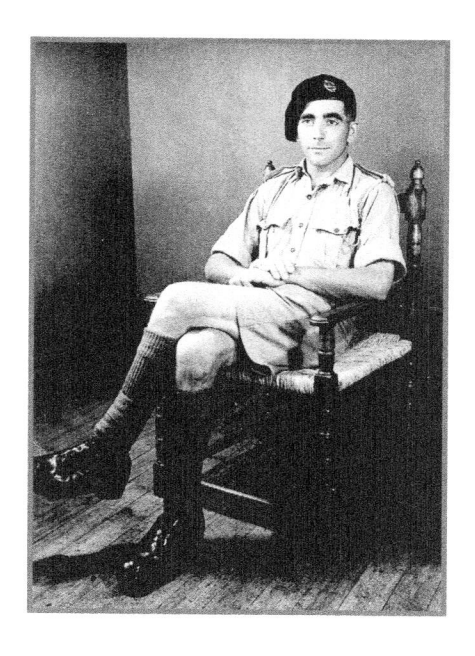

Wally was proud to serve in the Royal Tank Regiment and survived WW2 without any physical injury. But five years of conflict took its toll on his mental health.

This is his story.

Edited by Julie Norton
(his neice)

Contents

Tradition	1
Early days	5
The Phoney War	42
Dunkirk	65
Rebuilding an army	79
Desert rats	140
Italy surrenders	187
Back to Blighty	213
Postscript	226
About the author	227

Foreword

TIME CANNOT heal amputation, nor can it heal brain scars. The first can be seen and excused, the sufferer helped. With the second, people say, "The neurotic bastard, doesn't he realise the war has been over for 30 years?" Actually he can, but those scars are with him till he dies. The amputee cannot grow a new arm, but a neurotic looks normal. Some types go through the most awful experiences without being affected, while others who may be alongside them suffer scars on their brain which are there for life. These people do not want sympathy; that makes them worse. They just need to talk about it. In the end their friends come to know it all and the only thing left to do, at least as far as I'm concerned, is to write a book. That's what I did.

J.W.H.
1975

Tradition

TO SOMEONE who has not been in the services, and to be specific in my case, the army, the *esprit de corps* invoked by the traditions and the history of any particular regiment can be surprising.

When I was a recruit in the Middlesex Regiment I had to learn the regiment's history. I suppose that now that the Middlesex has been melded with two other regiments into one new unit[1], recruits will learn the histories of all three.

These traditions have come down through the years and some are even older than the regiments themselves. A soldier was originally a man who fought for pay, in contrast to the man who, as a serf bonded to a lord, had no choice. The soldier was a free man who could look the lord straight in the eye while the serf had to cast his eyes down. This right has been asserted ever since, but as is the way with some traditions, the whole thing has been reversed.

If a man does not look in the eyes of the person he is saluting, he can be charged with slackness. On the other

---

[1] *In December 1966 the Middlesex Regiment was amalgamated with the other regiments of the Home Counties Brigade: the Queen's Royal Surrey Regiment, the Queen's Own Buffs, The Royal Kent Regiment and the Royal Sussex Regiment, to form the Queen's Regiment. This then merged in September 1992 with the Royal Hampshire Regiment to form the Princess of Wales's Royal Regiment (Queen's and Royal Hampshires).*

Tradition

Wally (standing second right) with his mates in 1935 in front of a Vickers Mk 2, an early tank used for training. The soldier on the left is most likely wearing a belt first issued in 1908.

hand, the cap-badge of the old Ordnance Corps showed a small cannon with cannon balls which were obviously too large, and this is said to be a reminder of a long ago battle when the balls were too big for the guns – a permanent disgrace which somehow became something to be proud of.

Every regiment had little examples like this in their history: the Scottish one where the men fled the battle in kilts, then were not allowed to wear them again and had to be satisfied with 'trews'; and the regiment that, though surrounded, fought back to back and were afterwards called the 'back to backs', and wore two cap badges, one at the front and one at the rear to prove it.

Men were proud of these things and though in these modern times, it may be hard to believe, such things

2 The Reservist

Tradition

made the man fight harder just for the honour of the regiment.

Two hundred years ago, the hard-pressed colonel of The Middlesex exhorted his men to "die hard". They did and, though the colonel was killed, the regiment won the day. That day was still held as the regimental holiday until the last war. If this new unit was suddenly just as sorely pressed, that old cry would be heard again and the men would respond.

And that's my view of the difference between the old cavalry and the one-war-old tanks corps. The cavalry just

A photo taken before 1935. The men are wearing pre/early WW2 uniforms and the tank is a Vickers Mk 2. Wally is second from the left and was second driver. The corporal driver, first on right in overalls, taught Wally to drive. They met again in the war when the corporal had become a sergeant major.

did not like the fact that they were now just a small part of this new corps and after Dunkirk, when they got the chance, any ex-Tank man serving with them was sent back to the new tank regiments, then being formed.

I was proud to serve in the Middlesex with its many battle honours emblazoned on the Colours and, though not really happy with the Cavalry, I appreciated their views. But despite their newness, the Tanks was the corps my heart was really in. It did not need battle honours. On every field of action the tanks were there. And mostly they were there first. In the field, we did not back up others. They backed us.

※ ※ ※

Early days

I JOINED the army just after the general strike of 1926. At the age of 17 I was earning 17 shillings and sixpence *[88p]* a week. There were over two million out of work and the army's offer of "14 shillings a week and all found" seemed marvellous. I could write plenty about peace time soldiering, the three years I had in the Infantry and the five years in the Royal Tank Corps[1]. But I am writing this mainly to get the war years off my chest.

I was still on reserve in 1939, so served through till 'VE-day'. I was sent home from Italy in 1944 as a neurotic – a neurosis induced by prolonged war strain – and I am hoping that it will help to write about it, even 30 years later. My experiences did not include anything very terrible[2], but perhaps a lot of pinpricks accumulate. Much of the war I enjoyed very much. I had never left England before and I saw France, Cape Town, Egypt, Cyrene, Tunis, Libya, Sicily (Etna), on the way, and Italy. I would have seen none of it otherwise. The credit cannot be measured; the debit is neurosis.

A younger brother[3] and I rejoined the Colours together. We travelled back to the Royal Tank Corps depot at Wool in Dorset on 4th September, 1939. We were both glad

---
[1] *Wally left the army in 1934 and rejoined as a reserve in 1939.*
[2] *Wally is being humble here. He witnessed many terrible things including seeing many of his mates die. - Ed.*
[3] *Arthur Henry, seven years younger.*

Early days

to be back, but we found it was not the same army. We thought we would be meeting old friends, but we had stood still. There was a line of non-commissioned officers watching us come in. One sergeant yelled and waved to me. He was the young driver I had handed my tank over to three years before. Tanks to us drivers were like ships to captains. I had nursed this man with last minute warnings and advice, wished him luck, and left the army. Now he was wearing three stripes and I was a trooper. It was natural. The army had become a cadre for a million men. They promoted the men they knew; they did not know that I was coming back.

No-one seemed to know what to do. Everything looked to be in a muddle, so my brother and I joined a game of solo whist taking place on the stage in the YMCA. The steward looked very surprised to see us when he opened at tea time.

By chance when we came out we saw a blackboard and easel on the grass and I found my name and number there. I was posted to a dragoon guard regiment at Colchester. It had just been mechanised. I saw my brother once more after that, while on four days leave from France. He was also on leave, before joining the Eighth Army. He was killed at Sidi-Rezegh, Africa[1].

[1] *Arthur died in November 1941, aged 25.*
[Wally's youngest brother, Ralph, saw little action – he was captured almost immediately by the Japanese and spent the rest of the war in a prisoner-of-war camp.- Ed.]

6 The Reservist

Early days

Wally (right) with his younger brother Arthur 'on manoeuvres' in September 1935.

In the first days after the declaration of war anyone in uniform was a hero. People looked at you and you liked it. There were other reservists 'Mecca-ing' at Liverpool Street Station. I knew some of these but there were none of my old mates. One man I remembered, a Yorkshireman, had been insulted by the regimental heavyweight champion in the course of his peacetime service. (The champ was also the base drummer, two cases of being unique in one man.) However, in a regiment of young men there were not too many heavies to choose from. There was much more skill in the lesser weights. My Yorkshireman, "Jammy", got up from his bed (a man's bed was his settee and workbench), hit the heavy once and put him out for 10 minutes.

Liverpool Street gave us the worst train it could find, with no corridor. No matter, you could almost spit on Colchester from London. The train puffed steadily on for three hours without stopping. Jammy wanted to relieve himself: no chance. He waited, hoping the urge would go away. It got so bad, with him rocking to and fro moaning, that it interrupted our conversation. We did not like talking anyhow, it seemed so heartless.

We tried to help: "Put it out of the window". He attempted to comply, lowering the strap window and leaning out. One man grasped his belt at the back as a safety precaution; all Yorkshiremen wore belts and braces

September 1935 at Catterick: Wally (centre) with two mates standing in front of a Vickers Medium tank Mk 2 (Confirmed by the registration number which is mentioned in the vehicles census.) They were made in the 1920s and obsolete by the start of the war. They saw some action early in the war in North Africa but they were way out of date by then so were used as static armoured pillboxes. Because of the loss of so many vehicles at Dunkirk, they were brought out of retirement to use as tank driver training vehicles and this photo most likely shows the trio under training in the UK carrying out basic maintenance (judging by the spanner and socket wrench held by some of the crew).

8 The Reservist

Early days

in those days, that's how you could recognise them. Jammy suddenly leaped back and huddled in the corner. He said one word: "station". The platform was crowded.

When agony overcame embarrassment, he tried the door, with the safety man holding on. We suffered with him for five minutes but it was no good.

"Not while it's moving", he said. We all sat in an uncomfortable silence for 20 minutes. Suddenly he whipped off his boot, used it twice and put it straight on again. From the look on his face you would have thought it was the first time he had ever felt relief. When we mentioned that he had replaced his boot soaking wet, he said "It does your feet good." Then we were at Colchester.

The Dragoons looked to me to be made up of all young men, and I was ten years older than most of them. There were also some of Mr Hoare-Belisha's[1] boys doing six months on approval; whoever heard of a six months recruit liking it?

The regiment was equipped with light tanks armed with a .303 and a .5 gun mounted together so that you could use either. They were so near the roof that they were a job to handle, especially the .5, which was really too heavy to use at all in that constricted space.

---

[1] *Leslie Hore-Belisha was Secretary of State for War from 1937–40. In May 1939, he passed the Military Training Act, which provided for six months of full-time military training, before participants entered the Reserve.*

Early days

These were the first tanks I had seen with powered turrets. Our old tanks had manually operated ones. Trying to swing the gun upwards when you were sideways on a hill was a killing job. These new turrets were from floor to roof. You stood inside and revolved with it. All kit, food, tools and ammunition were packed in the corners. Anything you needed was reached through apertures. When the guns had been swivelled a couple of times and then a piece of equipment was wanted, the joke was to find it. Just try a little experiment: stand a broom up with one hand holding the top, shut your eyes, walk round the broom three times, then leave go and with your eyes still closed, walk straight to some nearby prearranged spot. If you could make the floor heave and rock at the same time, that would give the idea, only a tank is noisier and hotter and bits of it hurt you.

The regiment was very 'cavalry' influenced and not mechanically inclined. I believe they really wanted to keep their horses. The officers had a horse-drawn coach beside the parade ground and went for afternoon drives in it. They also mounted the tanks with spurs and riding crops and stood on the running board outside. One captain still used the same method to inspect tanks as he had used to inspect horses: he rubbed his white glove along the side.

As the tanks' maximum speed was 45 miles per hour, I was interested to see that they were driven at 40 miles an

Early days

hour on the road. The rule used to be half the maximum, else the rear vehicles straggled farther and farther back. When we made a roadside halt, the tank I was in hit the one in front. All the sergeant major said was, "You want to be more careful." I had thought there would be an instant charge and maybe a court of inquiry.

I was to be a wireless operator despite the fact that I had been sent there as a driver mechanic, first class, but that did not matter. The theory was that if you were one, you were capable of learning the other. Although for the first three or four months of the war I tried hard, I hated wireless telegraphy, and though I attained a speed of six words a minute at morse code, I never did master the rest of it.

Driving was odd. The engines were Rolls Royce, but I was used to driving a tank that was eight feet wide, sitting on the extreme right. The driver only saw straight ahead and had to judge the width. These tanks were six feet, six inches wide, and the driver sat on the extreme left. I had to adjust to a difference of about 12 feet. Later, in France, driving at the same 40 miles per hour, I missed telegraph poles by inches.

Back at Colchester however, everything was dead secret. To stop our movements being reported to Hitler, we left camp once a week *[as a trial run]*. Men who had wives in quarters were told to say goodbye to them. But we would drive away and get back in time for tea. Each time we went, everything was checked and handed over. One day we went as usual but before handing over the tank hangars, the quartermaster asked me to steal a fire extinguisher from the next hangar as he was one short. With an eye to promotion, and to stop him worrying throughout the war, I did this and we were finally on our way.

We were some miles along the road to Avonmouth before we realised that this was IT *[the real thing]*. My tank commander and I were sightseeing, when he suddenly broke down. He realised we had gone further than usual, and that morning he had not given his wife a proper farewell. It had been a wonderful year for fruit and my wife had a cupboard full of jam she had made which eventually went rotten, since she went home to her mother for the duration.

Strangely enough, the local people obviously knew. The route was lined with people who offered us all manner of fruits, cakes and drinks. How did they know? I supposed that special route was only used for actual departure. No-one had offered us anything before and this continued right across the country. Hitler's spies probably knew it as well.

A curious change came over my mate. Half an hour after his upset over his wife he was a changed man. He was a full corporal and a likeable man. I lost sight of him in France but we got on all right for the few months we

Early days

knew each other. The roadside offerings had made him realise that he was practically a single man again, and he was going to France too. Lovely!

"That's a nice bit," he remarked of one young lady. I reminded him of how he had felt half an hour ago and he said one had to look at things as they were. He was a practical man.

We boarded an Isle of Man packet. I had never been to sea before and wondered whether I'd be sick but I found the brag *[gambling card game]* school and forgot all about sea-sickness. Nearly everyone on the boat was sick except me. We were on the boat three days and I won quite a bit of money. Where it went to, I do not know, but we finished up at St Nazaire[1]. There was a kind of promontory alongside as we went to the anchorage.

As the boat came to the quay, Big Frank, who had not been sick throughout the voyage, suddenly lost his false teeth over the side. As they went down we saw the boat grind them against the quay wall.

[1] *Two and a half years later, on 28 March 1942, while Wally was in Africa, the Royal Navy and British Commandos undertook the St Nazaire Raid or Operation Chariot, a successful amphibious attack on St Nazaire's heavily defended dry dock. The destroyer HMS Campbeltown, plus 18 smaller craft, crossed the English Channel and was rammed into the Normandie dock gates. The ship had been packed with delayed-action explosives that detonated later that day, putting the dock out of service for the remainder of the war. This forced any large German warship in need of repairs to return home via the English Channel or the GIUK gap, both heavily defended by British units.*

Early days

The locals were lining the quayside in strength to welcome us. The younger women wore white lace caps for the occasion. Somebody said that was to tell you they were the town's virgins. There were many without caps.

We spent three days there. I was on guard duty first night. Dusty, my tank commander, was the guard commander. It was a camp of tents with no provision for the guard. It poured with rain all night and it was 3rd October, my 30th birthday. We chose the only partial shelter there was, a small haystack. It was too wet to sit down so the off-duty guard leaned on the lee side and the sentry stood at the other.

Everyone who has served in the army knows about the orderly officer. He is supposed to come round some time during the night and make sure that the guard is not sound asleep. In peacetime it was generally easy to judge when he would come as the mess closed at 11pm and he would be round soon after, ensuring himself a night's kip. Here it was different. There was a fifth column[1] scare. He could come round any time, and the orderly officer happened to be that over-regimental captain who used to rub the tanks with his gloved hand. We were armed with revolvers, and a revolver is not all that accurate, especially at night in pouring rain. This fool

---

[1] *A group of people, or spies, who undermine a larger group from within, usually in favour of an enemy group or nation, in this case the Nazis.*

Early days

came creeping round the tents while I was on guard. He was wearing a light mac which blended with the colour of the tents. I challenged him and, instead of answering, he dodged behind a tent. Of course I knew who it was but supposing I had been one of the younger men? We had been warned of these fifth columnists, and a panicky soldier on the first night in a strange country might have fired.

When he appeared next time I had my revolver out and pointed it at him. "If you don't answer this time," I said, "I will shoot you." It was such a stinking night that I meant it. This time he called me by name and that was that. The next morning the sergeant major called me over and asked me to explain. I told him that the only thing that stopped me firing was the fact that the captain was standing in front of a tent and if I had missed, someone else might have got hurt. (Twenty years or so later I saw a photograph in the paper of his two daughters. They could not have been born then.)

We moved from here up to Pas du Nord where we stopped until Dunkirk. I was learning morse code all the time. The tanks were usually parked in farms and they seemed to be laid out all in the same way. Built round three sides of a square, the left leg was mostly a café, the middle the farmhouse and the other leg the pigs' quarters with a dry loft above. These were generally our billets and were they cold! The floors of the lofts

Early days

were made of cement and there was always a six inch space between sloping roof and floor, for airing the hay I guessed. When you lay down, with no mattress, the wind would blow straight through.

For protection we shielded our beds with the wooden boxes that the petrol tins were packed in. These boxes were also handy as lockers, but we always had to be ready to go at a moment's notice. We had plenty of practice at moving out. On the alarm being given, all kit had to be packed, stowed on the tanks, tanks started up and driven to the moving off area no matter what was happening at the time: meals, morse, sleep, day or night. We could do it in 20 minutes and I was getting quite proud of my regiment's efficiency.

In England, we tank reservists had tried to insist that we wear our berets, which were a battle honour, but the regiment insisted that we wear the stupid side hats *[see photo on bottom of page 40]* which blew off or fell off as soon as you were near a tank. We still had a great esprit de corps for our old tank regiments. If out and about off duty we took off our side hats and wore our berets.

The off-duty periods were not many though. There was nowhere to go and the rule, because of the 'on call', was that we could go to the cafés of the village we happened to be in if we did not cross a road. One runner went each way round the block and all were warned. It was a good system but it could boomerang. Sitting in a café one day,

Early days

while we were learning morse there, one young soldier became involved in an argument with the sergeant major. It got very heated and the sergeant major reprimanded the lad about his insolence, quite legitimately too. The boy asked him what he could do about it as we were all confined to camp in any case. "Anyhow," he said, and this is what made us laugh, "I am time-expired and want my ticket." It turned out that he was one of Hore-Belisha's boys and had finished his six months. In the event when we moved nearer the danger area he was sent back to base as too young for the front line.

We were in billets at a farm at a place called Cambrin for about three weeks. The yard formed by the three sides was always thick with mud. There was a flight of stone steps to the café door and there seemed to be a daily delivery of beer. As most of the French men were said to be in the Maginot Line[1], it was mostly young women, their mothers and old men who ran things. The ma'm'selle who ran the café used to accept the delivery and go in to get the note signed while the driver relieved himself from the top step. She always came out again before he had finished and would wait politely with the note in her hand. He would re-dress, take the note with one hand, raise his hat with the other, wish the girl "Bonjour", and depart. I had always been told that the

[1] *The Maginot Line was a vast fortification that spread along the French/German border but became a military liability when the Germans attacked France in the spring of 1940.*

Early days

French were polite.

The yard had a brick wall, two feet high, forming a square in its centre. This was a swill dump which came in handy at meal times. We used to sit on the wall and when we had soya bean sausages for breakfast we threw them straight into the swill.

The loft itself was rat-infested. Every night one very large old rat used to come down a rafter from the roof. The rafter was near to Dusty's bed so he was more worried than the rest of us. He saw the old farmer and was given a huge trap, a good three feet long. The bait had to go in the middle; he put some cheese in it. It was gone next day but he didn't catch the rat.

There was no running water in this part of France. All I ever saw in the hamlets were communal pumps out in the open. The winter was very severe and the pumps were often frozen. We mostly managed to heat enough water for shaving by drawing it overnight, but sometimes we all had to wait till the cooks had thawed the pump with petrol heaters, and drawn off what they needed before we could wash.

One day we were all taken to Armentieres for a bath. For some reason, because the 1914-18 war song[1] had made the place practically immortal, I had imagined a pretty little village full of very eligible young women. It

[1] *"Mademoiselle from Armentières"* was a song that was particularly popular during World War I.

Early days

was a dismal little mining community with sleet falling and a high, cold wind.

There was not a soul to be seen and we went straight to the pit-head baths. At this time none of us knew any of the language except the few necessary phrases needed to contact a young lady, and the bath attendant was an old man, probably on a pension from the mine. He knew no English.

The 'baths' were actually showers placed centrally in a hall that had open cubicles round the walls. The floor was covered in damp coal dust as far as the cubicles, and under the showers there were little bits of well washed coal. The one was dirty to stand on, the other awkward.

The attendant shouted something to us in French, gave us two minutes to undress, then turned the water on, all the showers together, whether full or empty. We did not know what he was saying and were enjoying a lovely preliminary lather-up when he turned the water off. No matter how we all cursed him, he ignored us and we had to wipe the soap off as best we could. Anyone who has tried to wipe soap out of his hair without water will appreciate the position. By the time we had walked back to our cubicles, our feet were sticky with coal dust which had to be wiped off with the towel.

About this time, a truck started to run into town once a week. It was called the "passion wagon", which was an apt name. But we did want to see something of the

Early days

country. The first glimpse of Arras that I had was a bridge into town. The bridge had a low white stone parapet and, after the mud, looked clean and civilised. Then I saw that the only civilian on it was a scruffy old Frenchman relieving himself straight over the parapet into the river. When in France, do as the French do. We became used to this.

We had to use the cafés to relieve ourselves, though we soon wished we could go somewhere else. The cafés each had a piece of drainpipe slanting down along the front of the shop window, and that was it. Standing on the pavement was not too bad: your back was towards any passer-by. But the customers could look straight through the window at you from the inside.

This was where I had my first language lesson. In the slump before the war I had tried to get work at ICI. There seemed to be a firm here with the same initials and I remarked on the branches they had. Then I learned it meant "here". In England the shops do not start their signs with "Here we sell". They just put "boots" or whatever it is.

These small French towns did not have very much to offer in the way of entertainment. I did see one queue of men and was naive enough to ask if they were lining up for a cinema. It was a "maison", and personally, I would not have the nerve to line up along the pavement with all the passing women knowing what I was waiting for.

Early days

One of these houses backed on to the river bank and my mate and I, walking by, heard in the dark a Frenchman talking to a girl who had obviously just left her job in the 'house'. In these places there was always a bar on the ground floor and on a mirror would be written in soap and in English "Twenty francs – ten for the House – ten for the girl". The Frenchman we heard was trying to get things on the cheap. He was offering 15 francs and the girl was replying, "Non, Monsieur, vous entrez la Maison. Moi, Je finis 8 heures[1]." We laughed, but I found that to these girls, it was only a job[2].

Later, while visiting a French home, my hostess had a visitor. They were old school friends. My hostess explained that her friend worked in a "Maison" and that was that. Neither appeared to see anything peculiar in it. The lads also found that in the villages there were none of the 'monkey parades' of England. The girls did not want to know. There was a place for that if that was what you wanted, why not go there? Why pick on me?

During the months of the "phoney" war[3] we found that we were moved on a system. As we had the fast light tanks we were generally put 20 or so miles back from the

---

[1] *"No, Sir, you go in the House. As for me, I've done my eight hours."*

[2] *The girls would have avoided assignations with lone customers knowing they had more protection inside the Maison - Ed.*

[3] *See page 42.*

Early days

border at a place that acted as a hub. Roads radiating from this hub led to various parts of the border. If Hitler scratched his nose and pointed, we could be there in under two hours. One of the places he must have pointed to was Tourcoing, a little town near Lille. We were rushed there one day and were camped in a school.

It was here that I made friends with a French family: Simone and Paul with their baby. Paul had been injured at sea in the first days of war, was now at home and could not walk. If he received a pension, it was very small and Simone took in our laundry. One day, sick of the eternal egg and chips in the cafés, I suggested to Dusty that we go to Simone and ask her to cook us a real supper for which we would pay. At first she did not like the idea of our paying but we managed to persuade her and we went there as many evenings as we could.
I made real friends of these people and from anywhere we happened to be within 30 miles, we used to visit. Our major even allowed us a two-day Christmas there. He took a risk doing that, but Dusty was a full corporal and he took a chance. The last time I saw that family was about a week before Dunkirk. Paul said, "Wally, look". He got up with the aid of two sticks, then dropped them and proudly made the three steps to the table unaided.

After the war Simone wrote to me, telling me that she had been in the Resistance, but Paul died shortly after Dunkirk and she had now married again. She enclosed a

Early days

photograph of a smart girl of about 18, who had been the baby of six months whom I had helped look after.

There was a lot of makeshift and improvisation in these first months of war. I have mentioned our usual farm quarters. In town it was different. We had a large schoolroom as sleeping and rest room, with the tanks parked on the kids' playground. The school was still open and while we messed about with the tanks and guns, the kids came out to play, the young women teachers meticulously keeping them away from us. The only trouble was that the toilets were at our end, one long shed facing the wall with the corrugated iron back towards us. The girls went round the back out of sight but the boys had to use the back of the iron shed. The young teacher in charge of the boys had them lined up with her holding the head of the queue. She let the first six or seven go to the wall and watched them. When one was finished, she let his place be filled, and if one squirmed too much he could jump the queue. She ignored us and showed no embarrassment.

During this period I had my first brush with authority. It was pay day. Francs were about 160 to the pound and we generally drew 200, but they were deducting 20 francs for "sports". I did not see the fun of this. To my mind the war would not last long, and our money was going to support the funds of a strange regiment. Also I did not like the manner of the taking. My enemy captain

Early days

was doing the honours at the pay table in the open air, and the quartermaster was sitting beside him reading out the next man's name and how much he was to be paid. He then added "less 20". No-one had the grace to explain what the "20" was for, and the men went up one after the other, saluted for their pay, signed for it, and went off 20 short. Of course they muttered about it and supposed it was for "sports".

The attitude of it all made me see red. Then it was my turn. I saluted correctly and waited for the right amount. The captain asked what the trouble was. I said I wanted the other 20 francs. He said I was not getting it. He said, "You will take the 180 and sign for it – and that's an order." This was just up my street. I smiled at him and said I would not sign until I had my correct pay. I could see he was annoyed, and wondered if he would be fool enough to put me under arrest. The quartermaster unsportingly came to his rescue. In an aside that the other lads could not hear he said, "You can't argue with that bloke, sir. You can't order him to sign his name." The captain slammed down the other 20 with bad grace, I thought. I still paid it though. The major came up to me casually the next day and had a little chat and asked me for the money. I had been winning at brag and offered him 100 francs, saying that I had never realised the regiment was so hard up. He was a different type of man, he smiled sweetly, thanked me and gave me 80

Early days

francs change.

In 1939, 200 francs was a lot of money. We felt like the Yanks did in 1917[1], "Kings among men". France had not yet come to its mercenary senses and things were still cheap. To give an idea, we saw posters advertising top and bottom dentures for 250 francs, about 30 shillings [£1.50p] the lot. Vin ordinaire was three francs a litre. Our boys were incredulous. The Frenchmen were drinking it like we drink beer, in beer glasses, and they did the same. After six francs' worth they were incapable.

In one café we frequented, one old man used to come in, look at us and laugh. He was a "carrot dese wheat" man [quatorze dix-huit[2]] which meant he had served in the previous war. He would look at the group of us and say "Anglais soldat - pas beaucoup intelligence[3]". We only understood the "intelligence" bit and kept him in "vino" for the rest of the evening. It took me several months in several villages to realise he was right. But as far as men who were away from their normal environment could be, we were happy enough. For about one shilling [5p] we could have egg and chips, wine and 20 Players[4].

In one village the old village pump was frozen first thing. We found a café right across the road from our

---

[1] The US army joined the allies in WW1 in the summer of 1917.
[2] 14/18.
[3] "English soldier – not very intelligent."
[4] Cigarettes.

Early days

muddy pig pens. We were more experienced now and instead of waiting in the cold for the pump to be thawed out, we went in the café. The Madame's husband was in the Maginot and she had two beautiful daughters and, with their help, was running the café with a barber shop in the back room. It was pathetic to see how the poor mother tried to keep her trade up and at the same time chaperone her two girls amongst us soldiers.

The poor woman had her work cut out serving coffee while her two daughters were shaving us in the back room. She was constantly flitting between the two rooms, though for the life of me I did not see how we could possibly take advantage of them at that time of day. We would have missed breakfast for one thing, and been late on parade for another. And she need not have opened at seven in the morning. The girl who shaved me each day always managed to shave round my lips first so that as soon as the opportunity occurred she could kiss me. The coffee cost one franc and so did the shave.

On the move again, we found we were just a few kilometres from Tourcoing. Dusty and I decided to go there and visit our friends. The weather was bitter, the road like an ice rink and our boots were studded with hobnails. On this move we had reached the end of the 'on call' run so, paradoxically, we were not confined to camp. Now France is a wider country than England. Instead of a similar A1 road *[now superceded by the M1]*

26 The Reservist

Early days

going from south to north there are, or were then, lots of secondary parallel roads. This seemed to make for enormous fields in between. In turn, this made bigger ditches and a lot of fields had to have little bridges to the field gates. When we were travelling and the road was flooded, the only guide to the road itself was the line of poplars at each side. I have seen a tank in one of these ditches with only its cupola showing above the ditchwater, and the tank was seven feet six inches high.

The road to Tourcoing was a deep-ditched one. It was all right going there in the light but coming back at night in the moonlight and frost, half drunk in hobnail boots, was a test of the homing instinct of the British soldier. As we staggered along this road one night, slipping as we went, I heard a voice coming from ground level. It was calling the regiment's name and then asking for "a tow". As we went past, I saw a man's head above the waterline in the ditch. He was too drunk to get out on his own, but he was in good voice as he shouted at us what a lousy lot we were for not helping. There were other groups behind. Whether he was ever rescued or not I never knew. The water was icy.

Meanwhile we were all picking up scraps of the language. Once, one man, being very thirsty, went to ask at a farmhouse for water. None of us could think what he should say, until one man had a brainwave. "Eau de cologne", he said, "'O' means 'water'". The sufferer went to the door and when the woman answered, he looked at her and said "O". She was puzzled, so he slapped his mouth and said it again. He then remembered his manners and said, "s'il vous plait" *[please]*. After several minutes of pantomime, she smiled (she was very obliging), rushed inside and came out with a bowl of water, soap and towel. He did not like to hurt her feelings so he washed himself.

A few months later I had difficulty with the language with my friend Simone in Tourcoing. I was trying to tell her that we could not come the following week as we would be on manoeuvres. But she could not understand until, having exhausted my French, I said in desperation, "Exercise". To my surprise she understood.

One of our moves took us to Bethune where I had my second brush with authority.

We moved up to the town in the pre-dawn dark. We waited with the tanks at the side of a road as it got light. I felt dirty and though there were no facilities for washing I thought I could manage a shave. I used water from my bottle and the red glass of the rear light as a mirror. By this time the schoolboys were out in strength followed by the girls. They all stood round and watched our every move. It was a main road with pavements and as usual we all wanted to relieve ourselves. It was ten o'clock before we did move, and by that time relief was the only thing most of us were thinking of. The delay was because

Early days

billets had to be arranged with the mayor. In due course we arrived at a pavilion in the middle of a sports field and were told to go inside and wait for a meal.

No-one could think about a meal. The pavilion's walls were all made of glass and the kids were now crowding round the windows. The only toilets in the place had been commandeered by the cooks as they were the only place with running water. The cookhouse could not be used as a lavatory.

The funny thing is that now, 30 years later, I cannot remember what happened. The sergeant major was a big-mouthed man. His nickname was "Bummer" which meant he was good at self praise. Knowing me as the 'Bolshevik[1]' type, he asked me quite proudly what I thought of the billets. I was still desperate to relieve myself, and when he spoke, I thought of my new little house in Sidcup (£695 then, £14,000 now[2]) and said, "The people who arranged this are a set of inefficient bastards."

A corporal who had been one of the arranging party took offence at this and struck me. We had a set-to and I was put in the guardroom; maybe I found relief there.

Bummer gave his evidence in front of the acting squadron leader (the major was on leave). I was not charged with striking an NCO, there were too many

[1] *Argumentative.*
[2] *In 1975.*

Early days

witnesses to where the first blow came from, but just with what I had said to Bummer. The sergeant major, as an afterthought, said, "I asked him if it *[Wally's angry comments]* included you, sir, and he said 'Yes'." What was the good of arguing? The officer glowered at me and remanded me for the commanding officer's judgement next day in the orderly room.

This was in a large private house still occupied by the family. The army had the front, the family the rear. The trial was held in the front room on the ground floor. This time, having me on the run, the sergeant major put in the bit about me saying that when I got home on leave I was going to tell Mr. Hore-Belisha how the regiment wasted petrol, by scrubbing equipment with it.

The commanding officer looked at me very coldly. He asked me if I would take his punishment. I knew he could only give me 28 days, and if I chose to be court-martialed it could be much more. I said I would. To my surprise he only gave me 14 days. He also said that because of my comments about the petrol, he would take care that while serving under him, I would not get to England *[on leave]*.

I was placed in the hall under escort and the RSM attempted to give me a lecture. I did not see why I had to put up with that and told him so. After all, I was as old as him and knew as much about the army as he did.

The attic was the improvised prison. He went up there

Early days

to where the provost sergeant was waiting, coming down a few minutes later. I was then conducted up to my home for the next two weeks. It was the best quarters I had been in since leaving England: dry, clean and warm.

When on field punishment there is no smoking, no pay, and it also means that the time period is deducted from your service. The provost sergeant was an old acquaintance of mine. We were both reservists, though this was the first time we had met during the war.

The provost sergeant, addressing me by my Christian name, asked me if I had any fags to sell him. As it happened, I had 250 Players just sent to me from home (it was the period between Christmas and New Year) so I was able to sell him some.

He told me that the RSM had come up to warn him he had a hard case coming up and he would have to be very tough or there would be trouble.

I asked him what we were going to do, and he said that after I had laid my kit out as expected, we would go round the town on "exercise".

The exercise consisted of marching round the nearest corner then strolling round the town till we came to the privately owned hot water baths. It cost one franc each and my friend paid. As usual the place was run by a young woman, and when we shouted for more hot water she would come and turn the taps. Unfortunately these taps were outside. But I do not think the free men *[those*

Early days

not imprisoned like Wally] got a bath.

The fact that the army had turned the attic into a prison did not deter the 12-year-old son of the house from coming up in the evenings to use a tool bench at one end. We started chatting as best we could. I was often on my own, as my escort, trusting me not to escape, would leave me to go out himself, and the boy and I got on very well. The second night he came up with a message from his mother inviting me down for supper. I used to do little jobs for her, and after a few days I got my escort in as well. The one job I would not do for her was to kill a chicken she wanted to cook. A trained soldier, taught to kill, and I baulked at a chicken! The boy killed it. He took his mother's not very sharp bread-knife, laid the bird carefully over the backyard drain and laboriously sawed off its head. She told me their surname was Fevrier so the boy had been named Janvier (Master January February).

On New Year's Eve my guard asked me to do him a favour. There were two of them, a sergeant and a trooper and they both wanted to go to a New Year's "do". The trouble was that they had no keys to the house as they were always on duty in turn. This time they would be out till well after midnight, so would I stay up and, when they whistled, come down and open the front door? Of course I agreed, after all I was not going anywhere. I heard the whistle about one in the morning and they handed me a

Early days

pint mug half full of rum. Yes, I drank it all.

New Year's Day dawned. The ground was covered with deep snow. At eight o'clock, the lads were all drilling in the snow wearing full equipment; it was the army's way of clearing hangovers.

Those two weeks passed pleasantly enough though my wife wrote that she had had her allowance stopped including her personal money, which was a separate calculation. She did recover it later.

After I was released we did not stay long in Bethune. Presuming that I had had a rough time upstairs the RSM asked me if I would listen to him now. When I told him "No", he left it at that. That RSM was quite a nice bloke really. I respected him; he had a difficult job which he did well.

Realising that we would soon be moving on, I went with another man to have a look at the town. It was Sunday morning. He showed me a road junction where there had been a fatal accident the previous day. A collision between an army lorry and a civilian car had resulted in a woman on the pavement being pushed through a shop window. The broken glass coming down had decapitated her. (Since the war I have run a small shop[1], and every time I see children playing nearby and running up to the shop window and banging on it, I rush out and drive

---

[1] *A secondhand furniture and bric-a-brac shop in Acton, West London.*

them off. Their mothers never seem to see the danger, but I always remember that guillotine effect on that Sunday morning walk in Bethune.)

No-one ever explained the French rules of the road to us. We all knew we had to drive on the other side of the road so I suppose it was thought that anything else would be picked up as we went along. In fact we all thought the French were mad drivers, going straight across main roads without seeming to look. What we did not know was that all roads were classed the same, and as everyone gave way to their right, it was only necessary to look one way.

Fifteen minutes after passing the junction where the accident had happened I experienced a feeling of panic. One is easily frightened of what is not understood and until the brain has mastered what is happening the fear remains. In this case we were about to cross a road. We had heard nothing, yet approaching us was a very small car. The road was slightly uphill and the thing was moving very slowly and quite silently. For a minute I stood transfixed. Surely in that low gear it would be making a noise? It was so closed in that I could not see a driver. The thing sort of flowed up the hill past us and then it became clear. It was a pedal-car, twin pedals at that, and the two old ladies inside were working hard trying to get to church on time.

I did not see much of the town and, after a few days,

Early days

we moved out, this time to Vimy, where the headquarters were. However, my squadron was stationed at a smaller village, a mile farther down the road. Because of this the RSM did not see much of me, though he had been issued with a motor cycle and used to get around a bit.

This time our billets were on the ground floor, in the stables, much warmer but smellier. The horses had brick stalls. We slept four in a stall; I was in the corner. The mortar had been worn out of the bricks and had never been re-pointed. I found that the mice used these spaces as walkways and they could get along them quite easily. They did not seem to mind us sharing their quarters, and I noticed that the more confident ones would cut the corner by jumping about the last six inches across it.

One Saturday night some of us got hold of an old private car to take us to Tourcoing. We were officially confined to the locality so we asked the driver to cover us with sacks until we were past Vimy, as the RSM looked in all vehicles. When we wanted to return it was foggy and our driver could not be found. It was nearly an impossible job to find a car for hire on a foggy Saturday midnight in wartime. However, a boy of about 18 took us back. We had to put him up till the morning and I gave up my bed corner for him as it was warmer. As we were settling down for the night, he started shouting. It took us some time to find out what the trouble was as none of us knew the French for mice. It was the mice short-cutting

Early days

the corner. They had never done it to me, but they were using his face as a stepping stone and shortening their journey round the corner.

Naturally we all had to see Vimy Ridge[1] and I believe we actually paraded for the visit. It was a long, gently sloping hill, covered now with a 20-year growth of scrub and small trees. At the summit was the stone memorial wall to 20,000 Canadians who had died in one day when they took it. I looked down the long slope. Every one of those men must have been visible all the way. The Germans, who, in my own experience, were humane as far as they could be, must have been sickened by the slaughter, and what was it for? Only half the top of the hill was won. I was surprised at the proximity of the opposing front lines: the width of an ordinary road! In between had been the two complexes of trenches with their cells and offices, just 30 yards, and where they had tried to blow each other up there was one long hole making the two lines of trenches appear to be on the edge of cliffs.

I also noticed the chains to the machine-guns on the German side. I wondered what kind of generals would conduct a war in that way. I hoped ours would be different.

I had my last go at authority at Vimy, at least my last

[1] *The Battle of Vimy Ridge was a military engagement fought as part of the Battle of Arras, in the Nord-Pas-de-Calais region, during WW1. There were four divisions of the Canadian Corps in the 1st Army, against three divisions of the German 6th Army.*

Early days

before Dunkirk. It was still bitter weather and I was with five others sent to the cookhouse for 'spud bashing' [peeling potatoes]. It was dark, as we were outside the building; it was also freezing cold. There were four one-hundredweight sacks of potatoes, three sacks of onions the same size and two of parsnips. I did not know how to peel parsnips. Potatoes are easy, you just keep cutting at them till there is nothing to cut and then throw what's left in your hand in a bath of cold water. The onions were different. They were frozen and after taking off one layer there was still more ice. With six men hacking away we could have finished in two hours, but the cook lance corporal, probably "unpaid" at that, called two men in to the nice warm cookhouse to wash dishes. That left four and of course the two inside preferred to stay where they were. Twenty minutes later he called another two in. That's when I stopped. In the argument that ensued, I said I would fetch the quartermaster. Then the lance corporal gave me an order not to leave the job. I left regardless, and the result was that the job was put back on its proper footing. I was still charged though; I had refused to obey a direct order, one of the most serious crimes in the army. I went in front of the major this time but the evidence of the quartermaster was in my favour. The major heard both sides and then sent the quartermaster and the sergeant major out. This left me and the cooks. Three of them were there to back each

Early days

other up. Then the major let them have it.

"I have told you before of this," he said. "You get extra money to do the job and try to set others to do it for you, and I'll have no more of it. Now get out, the lot of you."

Then he turned to me.

"Now Harmer," he said, "you got field punishment while I was on leave, on a bloody silly charge, and now you are in here on this. When the war really starts, do you want some of these bloody fools in charge of you? Or would you sooner be in charge of them? I will give you the choice. You can either have a stripe or seven days."

I took the stripe and came out of that situation a lance corporal. The next time the RSM saw me he nearly fell off his bike.

As the colonel did not quash my appointment I presumed he must have thought better of his threat, and I was shortly to go on leave. An appointment, by the way, is not a promotion. It is a kind of half-way mark up the first rung. Historically, a horseman was superior to a foot soldier and was armed with a lance, a horseman's weapon. Even if the lancer lost his horse, as long as he retained his lance he was still superior. A lance rank really means one belongs to the rank below. In the same way, a lance sergeant is only a corporal. Then there are even degrees within the appointment: lance, unpaid lance, acting unpaid lance and, lowest of the lot, temporary acting unpaid lance. When you rise to that fourth lowest

Early days

position you generally go up.

One evening I took the half-mile walk up to Vimy for my leave pass. There was a lorry load of us and we each had to lug every bit of equipment with us: full marching order, kitbag, gas mask and tin hat.

The leave office was in a small shop and we leaned against the shop window while we were waiting. After a time we all needed to relieve ourselves but were frightened to leave the vicinity in case something happened while we were absent. We all stood with our backs to the window and relieved ourselves across the pavement. That was when a woman came along. She stood as near the window as she could, but held her coat back. When the pavement was clear she went on.

We were driven to Boulogne, where we would board the boat home, some time during the evening. How is it that someone always knows the procedure? There we were with half a ton of kit strapped and slung around our persons and, with a lot of other sheep, we were told to form up and march to the camp. I suspect that some 14/18 man had told his son about that place as I am sure the French had left it alone since then.

As we straggled through the town more like today's 'hippies'[1] than soldiers, I noticed that some men were dropping out of the ranks and going into the cafés. I

---

[1] *Members of a youth movement in the late 1960s who wore their hair long, grew beards and rebelled against convention.*

Early days

marched on. Those idiots were jeopardising their leave for the sake of a drink. What bloody fools! We struggled up the hill. I think the highest point must have been selected in case of attack. When we reached it we saw that the camp was a shed, filled with double tiered bunks with wire netting for springs and no mattresses. We each carried one blanket, but it was too cold to lie down.

We could buy cigarettes here without paying duty but we could do that in town. We could not go to bed in any case. There was a board and easel where it was written, 'Watch this board for the parade time'. I am sure some temporary acting unpaid lance corporal crept out and silently wrote the time on the board, because suddenly the time was there. I did not see the reason for secrecy as the time of the tides would be known to Jerry.

Wally (left), his wife Isabel and brother Arthur, pictured while on leave from France prior to Dunkirk. Wally is wearing the uniform of 5th Iniskillins Dragoon Guards. They never saw Arthur again. He died in action in November 1941, aged 25.

Early days

We all struggled into our kit again and marched down town for the boat. As we passed the cafés the "bloody fellows" noted our passing, and finishing off their drinks, slipped into the ranks again.

So back home for ten days! This was the last time I should see my brother. He stayed with my wife and me for those few days. We both went back to France. I did get one letter from him written at Dunkirk time. It simply said "Keep alive".

The Phoney War[1]

THERE ARE various way of getting promotion. One is to be terribly efficient and work very hard. This way only gets you so far, as sooner or later a niche is arrived at in which you fit so nicely that you can never be spared for higher things. In peacetime, if you were good at any particular sport, that was a certain way up the ladder, as the regiment wanted your skill representing it on the field. I knew a man who had been to public school and was a good pianist. He used to entertain us on the NAAFI piano till the corporals realised how well his playing would sound in their mess, and he went up a step. When the corporals had the sergeants round in the usual way, about once a month, the sergeants heard what they were missing. He finished up with a commission.

One can also move up by being so useless at the job that the best way out is to promote you. But the simplest way is not to look for anything at all. If you can do the job and be a thorn in the side of everyone over you they get rid of you. This is what happened to me.

A new unit was being formed. The regiment was

---

[1] The 'Phoney War' was an eight month period at the start of WW2, during which there was only one limited military land operation on the Western Front, when French troops invaded Germany's Saar district. The Phoney period began with the declaration of war by Great Britain and France against Nazi Germany on 3 September 1939, and ended with the German attack on France and the Low Countries on 10 May 1940.

The Phoney War

to supply a man or NCO *[non-commissioned officer]* capable of being a tank driving sergeant. I was selected for this. A cook was also required and there was a suitable man who had been given some field punishment just after I had mine. We were both strongly recommended. The way things were done does not really make sense. The regiment was on the move and my squadron, half a mile down the road from the main body in Vimy, was packed up, lined up, and started up. Everyone was aboard his respective vehicle. Every man's kitbag and back pack had been left outside his billet for the baggage truck to collect. The truck was even now doing its rounds, someone throwing it all in, in one big heap. It was seven in the morning.

Word came for me to dismount, get my kit and join the Second Armoured Reconnaissance Brigade's HQ. I had never heard of this lot, nor had anyone else, but there was no time to reflect on that. I had to find the baggage truck before my kit was lost for ever. In it I had two new pairs of pyjamas my wife had just sent me, two mattress covers which I used on alternate weeks as sheets, and my chess set. I did not want to lose any of this. I found the truck at one of its stops, climbed over the tailboard and started searching.

Kitbags and packs were still being thrown in and then the thrown-out cook got in as well. While we were inside, the truck rushed off over bumpy little ways, stopped, loaded on some more and swung round to somewhere else. It was half light outside and nearly dark inside but we both found our kit in under ten minutes. We threw it out, jumped off, collected it, went back to where the squadron was moving out and looked for someone to give us instructions.

The sergeant major (Bummer) was last in a bren-gun carrier, and as he went past I shouted, 'Where do we go?" He shouted back "Buggered if I know," and then laughed his head off.

That was goodbye to the horse guards. I now remembered that in the scramble of the first message telling us to leave the regiment it had been mentioned that I was to be a sergeant. I looked at the only man I knew in the whole of France and suggested we walk up to Vimy as at least we could get a coffee there and someone might see us.

We picked up all our kit and walked the half mile. I only then realised it was uphill. Walking along Vimy high street, I noticed an English soldier standing in a doorway. As he was the only one in the place, I approached him with a view to finding out if he knew anything. He asked us if we had come to join this new unit. It turned out that he was to be the sergeant major, and we were his first recruits. While the sergeant major waited for his unit to build up the three of us lived in a hotel in Vimy for three days, the best three days I had had in France as far as billets were concerned, with all meals served in the hotel. During that time about 100 men arrived of various ranks, from trooper to lance sergeant. Amongst these was a lance corporal whom I will call "Bill" and his trooper mate. They had heard there was going to be some rapid promotion, and after a few minutes acquaintance, while the three of us were together in a little room, they sang a song. I no longer remember the words except that each verse finished with "I'm a little man with big ideas". They probably thought that before the day was out they would both be brigade majors.

We then moved to a big country house in its own grounds, where the unit commander, a brigadier, had arrived. He ordered all his unit to parade in one long line and interrogated each man in turn. He was a good man and in the short time that was to be at his disposal (three weeks later Hitler came round the Maginot Line), he contrived to have an efficient unit, if not very experienced. This is taking into account that he must have known enough about army ways to realise what type of men his personnel comprised.

It was a bit pathetic to hear the way some of the men answered his questions. They were telling him how good they were at everything and he was listening. I suppose he was wondering how their previous bosses had possibly been able to spare them. He promoted lance corporal Bill to full sergeant in charge of radio. As

The Phoney War

usual, when he confronted me I was perverse. I handed him my record book. "It's all in there, sir", I said. And it was. Everything I had ever done in the army, peace or war, was in there and everything was marked, "Pass First Class". He read it through and said I would be sergeant in charge of tanks on the driving and maintenance side. The promotion was backdated to two weeks before my release from field punishment, so in effect that meant that at the time of the row over potato peeling, I was receiving a sergeant's pay.

During the next few days things happened in a mad rush. The men who formed the bulk of the unit were new from home. For the most part they could not drive tanks though they were proficient on trucks. I only wanted six but they had to be taught and selected.

While I was all day on this work Sergeant Bill was equally hard at it on the radio side. In the middle of it all I was sent to a small town to learn to drive a new vehicle: the scout car. It was a three day course and the officer in charge knew his work. He was a lieutenant and assumed we all knew something about our job. He showed us the mechanics of the car in two hours, and it was a beautiful little piece of work.

With a four-wheel drive, the half-shafts went from a central differential in an 'X' formation to the wheels. The differential itself was no bigger than my two cupped hands. It had five forward gears epicyclic, or pre-selector, and a master lever that put the whole lot in reverse. The idea was that if the enemy was sighted and there was no room or time to turn, it could shoot backwards nearly as fast as forwards. At the same time, the steering would change from the front four wheels to the back two. The thing weighed about three and a quarter tons, had a Daimler engine and good armour plating. It had four wheel brakes that could stop it within its own length, and in forward gear could reach 70 miles an hour. In reverse it would still do over 60, and the seat was placed diagonally to help the driver see all round.

The village school had a sports field and we used the track to get accustomed to the scout car. The lieutenant said any bloody fool could drive forward and sent us all round in reverse. After an hour he thought we were good enough to go round the town. That was a laugh. The car looked more or less the same either end, and we drove among the traffic and trams in reverse. Because of this there was a tendency to cut other vehicles up, and we were still not used to driving on the right hand side; the tram drivers were especially annoyed. But that three day course taught me to drive a vehicle which I was to see a lot of later on. Thirty years on I see the only improvement to this car is a turret on top; the first ones were flat-topped.

Back at the reconnaissance HQ the mad rush continued. I now had five of my six drivers and a choice of two men to make my complement complete. One of these approached me one evening and asked for the job. His argument was that the other man was as good as him, but he wanted the job. Although there was a certain amount of prestige in being a tank driver, it was also known to be the next most dangerous place to be after the tank commander. I felt that if he was keen enough to ask, he might just as well have the job, other things being equal. So I gave it to him.

A few days later we were in Arras, with Jerry all round us, and his tank went out on a solitary foray. It didn't came back. Whether the crew was killed or captured I never knew, but this created a little worry that grew as the war progressed. Someone had to drive the tanks and someone had to teach them. Two years later in the desert my squadron leader said to me, "Sergeant, we lost eight drivers in that do. Do you think you can get another eight by the end of this week?" This gave me the impression that I was training men to be killed. (This little worry became a big anxiety by the time we reached Naples and it was just after that that I was sent home ill.) *[With mental health problems. See page 216.]*

We were now enjoying our last few days of the "phoney war" though we did not know it. Our billets were still only half a mile from Vimy. We could take a short cut to it across the fields and went there in off periods to have a drink and pass the time. I was there with a pal drinking coffee one day and, although he was quite a personable man, he had only one tooth left in his upper set and that was right in the middle. We were sitting at a table minding our own business when suddenly a feminine voice behind us said slowly and distinctly, "You are a lovely boy". We both swung round to see which one of us she was referring to, and it was my pal. She was a nice kid of about 16. When my friend found he was the choice he threw his head back, opened his mouth wide and laughed the place down. He was entirely unselfconscious about his tooth, and so was she. Her sister was running the place while her husband was "in the Maginot", and the younger one was trying out her phrases on any likely lad she picked.

Not long after that I cut across the fields and a small wood, and was apprehended at rifle point by some infantry men who had arrived in the area. They were not satisfied with any of my documents and marched me at gun point to their HQ. After some discussion they let me go, saying that as far as they had known there were no other soldiers in the vicinity and all strangers to them were potential fifth columnists. They did not even know that Vimy was five minutes away.

It was five o'clock on a Sunday morning in the second week of May, a lovely day and the sun was shining into our room. No-one was up. Then there was a sudden chatter of machine guns and the zoom of an aircraft.

The Phoney War

Everyone woke in amazement. Had some fool lost his mind? Fancy shooting up a peaceful village like that! He might have killed someone.

That was the end of the phoney war. The street was full of spent cases which we collected as souvenirs. They were the only shots fired that day. It looked as if Jerry were warning us.

If that was the end of the beginning, things nevertheless seemed to progress fairly casually. We moved out on to the Arras road, taking up positions defending a little bridge which took the road over a small river. We were told that two enemy armoured cars had broken through the French defence system and we were to watch out for them. What fools these people must have been! What chance had they got? What could be accomplished by two cars with the strength of the French and our own force against them?

I did not care for the disposition of our six tanks though. We were all equipped with a searchlight on the turret, the beam hand-directed by the tank commander, which meant that his head and shoulders were out of the tank. And that had to be me. When anything came over the bridge I was to shine my light on it and dazzle the gunner while the others shot it to pieces. He would be bound to go for my light as he would not see anything else.

However, nothing came on. The sergeant major had

befriended the farm people nearby and when it was decided that we had been there long enough, we went back towards Arras. Two women from the farm decided to take the opportunity to leave at the same time and, amid much laughter, rode out of the danger zone on the sergeant major's tank.

We did not reach Arras, but stopped on the same road again. I was left for the night at the side while the rest went to other positions. I did not know where any of them were, nor how to contact anybody, as by now there was radio silence. I guessed I was there as first sentry. I stayed there for 36 hours; rations came up but no news.

My position at the side of this road, with my back to Arras, was about three miles outside the town. On my left there was a valley. On the right 50 yards up the road was a café on the corner. Standing up in that turret all day, I watched the refugees coming along to what they thought was the safety of the town. They were mostly travelling in big horse-drawn carts, head to tail, too big and heavy for just one horse; there should have been at least two. Each cart was loaded with people and their bedding. Getting down to essentials, I suppose a mattress and blankets are the priority. Every so often things were thrown off to make room for more people. No-one worried about the horses. It was quite warm and how far they had travelled I do not know, but some of these heavily-laden animals were on their last walk. I saw several that were walking in slow motion: one pace a second.

There was a sudden diversion with aircraft and machine guns. There were 20 or more of them zooming along the valley back towards the front. They were actually lower down than I was. There was no answering fire and they were well out of my range.

Strangely enough, the café owner did not seem to be in a hurry to move out. Whether it was because of a sympathy for his fellow men who called in on their way, or whether he was doing such a trade that he could not bear to abandon it was a moot point. There was a dog at the place, a small black dog, and it could open the door from either side; it was in and out a lot.

An Alsatian dog came down the road on its own. I would not like to see another like it; like the horses, it had come too far. It was walking on its knees and could not find the energy to go past the café and lie down. The little dog saw it and became practically human. I watched it as it went into the shop and barked until it received attention. In the end the man came out, saw what was needed and brought out water and food. The Alsatian stayed there that day.

We did not reach Arras until the next Sunday. We were supposed to be defending the town. It was a beautiful morning and we arrived at a smart residential street about six o'clock. The street was quiet, not a soul was about. Immediately we set about making road blocks.

The Phoney War

Two big iron gates were pushed away from a wall with the help of a tank, and a couple of cars were turned on their sides. Suddenly windows were going up, heads coming out and the rush started. Families came out, cases shoved in their cars, and they were gone. It took just 60 minutes for that road to be converted from a quiet peacetime suburb, with everyone having their Sunday morning lie-in, to a war zone with no-one in it except us.

One of the houses had a castellated top around a flat roof. The sergeant major decided it would make an ideal position for himself with a bren gun. He went up there to literally hold the fort. I went round the town with a lieutenant and some men, making more road blocks. One car we took, quite a good one, was hard to get into.

It took a surprising time to break the windows, even with a crowbar. While we were doing it, the owner arrived and went on his knees beside me pleading for his car. After five minutes of it I got fed up and said to the lieutenant, "Oh let him have it, we can take another."

The lieutenant said, "Sergeant, there's a war on." That was the first time I had heard that phrase, although later it became everyone's excuse for everything: inefficiency, rudeness and just plain laziness. The most hated four words in the language.

Later that day we experienced our first bombs. They were incendiaries and the sergeant major, gallantly at his post, fired the bren gun. The pilot looked at him,

The Reservist 53

The Phoney War

turned round and threw him a handful onto the roof, all for the sergeant major. That sergeant major was a brave man and a good soldier. With his rank he had no need to pick himself a job like that. In the excitement of the moment, he jumped straight off the roof. It was a two-storey building and he landed on his army boots! He then remembered the gun and went up to the roof again to rescue it.

We had no way of putting out fires. There did not seem to be any water under pressure. If there had been originally then Jerry must have bombed the water tanks. I watched a street of terraced houses burn one day and thought of the London rules of building. One house caught, the fire went to the roof, the main beam of the roof caught and as it went through the party wall to the next house, the fire went through too. Hot embers from the beam dropped down and so the house burned down from the top. One pail of water would have stopped it at that party wall, but we did not have it.

No rations were coming through so we had to go out on foraging parties. A lieutenant, six men and I went to the grocery shops to see what we could find. They stocked a lot of rusk-type bread which was wrapped and did not seem to go stale. A lot of the shops had already been broken into. We went into the tobacconist but we did not want the French smokes. One shop had a heap of pipes on the floor but, although I am a pipe-smoker, they were of no use to me, being very small-bowled. I was silly enough not to allow my men to take anything that was not essential. I suppose Jerry later took what he wanted or it was burned.

The town was now being bombed continually and we were taken into buildings for safety. We were also being sniped at and, as this was our first taste of war, it was strange that no-one seemed to worry about the bullets. They always missed and we became used to hearing the whang of a bullet as it went past. That was something I taught my men later on: the difference between firing on the level and up or down. A gun has sights that can be altered as the range differs. The farther aimed, the higher the trajectory. How does that work out if you are sniping from the belfry tower of a church at a target at ground level, or shooting at a target on a tower when you are down below? The gun-sight is bound to be wrong.

There were some attempts to catch these snipers but it was futile as they were firing from buildings that overlooked us yet were several streets away. We also found out that there were a lot of hidden underground passages where they could make their escape. These people did not even have to break cover.

I had never had much to do with the chief clerk of the unit. One day he took me to one side. He had sergeant major's rank and, as head man in the orderly room under the officers, he would get to hear things. He told me that

The Phoney War

the Germans had gone round Arras and were now up to the English Channel. I did not really believe him though what he said was somewhere near the truth. He then said, "I should not be here surrounded like this. I am officially a noncombatant and it's not right." Officially he was quite right; he should not have been there. He was one of the very few cowards I met during the war.

I got tired of the bombing. For the most part I sat and smoked and slept in a cellar full of men underneath a large house. There was a fanlight at pavement level and in front of it was a row of sandbags. Every time a bomb fell nearby, the sandbags jumped up and came down again. Every time they came down they split a bit more, and more sand came out.

I had not slept for a long while and my perversity won again. "If anyone wants me I will be upstairs", I said. The house was five storeys high and I went to the top. I found a woman's room with a wardrobe the width of one wall. This was open and full of evening dresses and fur coats, and there was a canary in a cage. He sung a bit when I came in and I looked to see if he had water and food. He had, so she could not have left him long. If she had left the cage open it would have done him no good. Maybe she got back to him in time as I expect the refugees soon crept back.

However, I undressed (the first time for a few days and the last for a few more as it turned out) got into her bed, sheets as well, and had a lovely four or five hours. Each bomb that fell rocked the old place but I was too sleepy to worry.

The next day, one of the men approached me. I did not know him personally but he was wanting a cover and I was a sergeant.

"Sarge," he said, "Do you know they have vacated the NAAFI and it is full of fags?" I did not know there was a NAAFI but, taking two of my own men and some empty sandbags, I let him lead us to it.

It was a café which looked as if someone had shouted "They are here!". Meals had been left half eaten; there must have been quite a few people in the place when whatever alarmed them made them leave. I could not see one cigarette.

"They are in the cellar, Sarge", the man said, and this confirmed my belief that he would not risk stealing them on his own. I struck a match and started down. There were sounds of someone else there before us. Putting on my best non-com voice, I asked who was there and received that silliest of answers, "It's me."

With an intellect like that I knew who was coming out on top. I struck another match and saw a guardsman in the process of filling his kitbag. I asked him what the hell he thought he was doing. He told me that he was only taking cleaning gear, and he was right: he had a kitbag full of metal polish and blanco. He had enough to make sure he'd be a clean guardsman for life so I excused him and he was thankful to escape.

Then we set to work. I took tobacco and the lads filled up with cartons of 200 cigarettes. I have often wondered if that guardsman was given his first stripe for taking that supply back to his colonel.

We were in Arras for about ten days. It was our baptismal period for what was to be. The tank I mentioned before was lost, and so was the popular sergeant major, the one who jumped from the roof. He was also the man I had seen in Vimy that first day. I was told he had been wounded in one of those little forays in which the tank was lost, had been picked up by a bren carrier[1] which then received a direct hit. I never did see the sense of these jaunts; we knew the enemy were all round us now, else why was there no communication with the outside? Also Jerry knew we were inside. What could have been the point of sending one light fighting vehicle out under fire?

Actually we were not quite encircled. It almost seemed that we had been left an escape path. There were two incidents during the night and day prior to going. The first was that we were told we could write letters, which would go in the morning (whether they ever went farther

[1] *The Universal Carrier, also known as the Bren Gun Carrier from the light machine gun armament describes a family of light armoured tracked vehicles built by Vickers-Armstrong and other companies.*

than the nearest fire I do not know) and the second involved me.

There were platoons of men doing outpost duty, some farther out than others. Tanks were detailed for the job of acting rearguard to them as they retired to the centre. It was one tank to each platoon. Sergeant Bill had one tank and I had another. My lot were about four miles along a road. It consisted of guards, and I was to give a message to the lieutenant in charge that I was to cover his retirement to Arras.

I found them occupying the last two houses in the road, one each side. I stopped in the middle of the road and as I dismounted, the lieutenant came smartly out from one of the houses and met me while I was still beside my tank. I gave him the message, that I was to cover his retirement into Arras at midnight. He nearly went mad.

"Sergeant, stand to attention," he shouted, "Do you know who you are talking to?" I was flabbergasted and it is not often I am at a loss for words. I did not see what he was getting at. Then he said loudly, for he wanted his men to hear, "**We are the Guards. We never retire.**" He was a "Well, this type can easily be dealt with" sort of man.

Two yards away my crew of two had been looking on with interest. They had heard it all. I saluted the officer, turned round to my men and shouted at them as if they were a hundred yards away, "**You heard what was said?**

The Phoney War

This officer is a guardsman, and they never retire."
I then turned back to him, gave him another salute and said, "Thank you, sir." He returned my salute and went away. Then I looked to see the best defence position I could take up.

Suddenly guardsmen appeared with huge rolls of barbed wire. One climbed on the tank, wrapped wire round the turret and jumped down. I asked him what he was doing and he said it was the officer's orders. They worked from the houses on both sides of the road, tying the barbed wire round the tank through the front door, up the stairs, out of a window, then the tank again, on to the other side of the road and so on. I went and found the lieutenant. I explained to him that I was not part of his sacrificial force, that if he did not go back at midnight I would leave him there, and that while I was with him he would have to leave the positioning of my tank to me.

I told him I had no intention of jeopardising either the tank or my crew, by being wired into the centre of the road. Telling my driver to start up, I said if he did not want his barbed wire all broken he might as well get it off the tank, as I was going to place it at the side of the house with the guns round the corner. I won that round and the wire came off. He left me alone till dusk then he told me that I was to shoot anybody who came up the road from now on as all his men were in.

At about ten o'clock I heard men marching up the road

The Phoney War

– army boots can be heard quite a distance away. There was no apparent secrecy about their movements and I could hear them talking. I could not believe it was Jerry and my two mates agreed. Telling them to cover me, I left the tank and crept along the hedge in the shadows; it was bright moonlight. I saw these men were on our side but as they approached I challenged them. The lance corporal in charge said they were coming in from outpost duty as their orders were to come in at ten. I accompanied them to the lieutenant and he admitted he had forgotten them.

Half an hour later when I was back on watch he approached me and asked what time was he to go back and what time did I make it. When I told him he said I was three minutes slow. A little later my crew saw two men coming up to us. While we were deciding whether to shoot or not, they went down one of the air raid shelters that had been dug in various places. Once again I went out; I had my revolver out each time. I crept down the stone steps; you can creep even in army boots if you want to; you put your heel down first. The shelter was lit by a candle and I could just see the two men. They looked like railwaymen coming off late turn. They were both about 60 and dressed in overalls.

There was no radio equipment nor anything else on view except a little kitchen table and two stools. They were sitting at the table crying. I left them there.

The Reservist

The Phoney War

What would you have done? They may have been fifth columnists or they may not. They were probably old timers from the 14-18 war. If they were the enemy there was nothing they could tell Jerry that he did not know already. Therefore I do not feel I dodged my duty, but if I had obeyed that idiot who would have had me shoot his own men and in cold blood, I would still have it on my mind.

Back at the tank at 11.30 the platoon's several trucks were lined up in front of the HQ. At 11.45 they were all started up. At 11.55 everyone was mounted and at 11.58 with the lieutenant checking by his (fast) watch, they moved out. I had been told to follow in 15 minutes, but the three of us felt disgusted. I said, "Well, after that let's not go in till one o'clock." And that's what we did and, without my saying anything, my driver did not once exceed ten miles an hour. I never saw that lot again.

We left Arras in the early morning. It was dark and over to my right I could hear a sergeant giving drill book instructions to his men, "Platoon at the enemy in front, five rounds - fire". I could not see nor hear any enemy. I was in a unit with vehicles in front and behind. We received no orders. Perhaps someone was trying to save the tanks at the expense of the infantry. We went on.

I was told to do a fire and retirement movement with Sergeant Bill's tank. It was now light and he was told to drive half a mile and take up a position and I was to go past and cover him. I saw no enemy but I knew that their tanks were armed with 88mm. guns (which we did not match until four years later in Italy). One of my stops was a small round haystack. I stayed in front of it. Behind it I was blind and at the side silhouetted. My tank was turned sideways with the engine running and the turret turned towards the enemy. Without any warning a shell burst 30 yards in front. There was no sound and I saw nothing. I heard the next one; it burst a little beyond the haystack.

"He has bracketed me", I thought, "time to go." I had not moved more than ten yards when a third shell hit the haystack, setting it alight.

The road went round a bend and that was the end of the exercise. I followed my partner, who had not stopped again, though it was not a mad rush. We just drove on until we were behind a miscellaneous collection of vehicles which were stopping and starting.

Then we were bombed and strafed from the air. Our turret held weapons that were not quick enough to follow aircraft. Everyone got out of his vehicle and we dived for cover under the tanks. There was another man with me under my tank and we saw the bullets hitting the road in front, then heard them run up the front. We both realised that if the angle of impact had been a little less, they would have ricochetted under the tank. Before the next lot came we had got back another foot. Then they dropped a few small bombs. As the second one came I remembered to unclench my teeth. No harm was done. I saw two men climb down from a tank armed with Bren guns. They were not tank men but had the only weapon that could have been of use. I realised that they had actually liked the situation; they had something to hit back with. There is nothing so demoralising as helplessness.

※ ※ ※

Dunkirk

WE SEEMED to go north, in and out of the French-Belgian border. Some people were in their doorways waving to us, whether in irony or sympathy we could not tell.

Daylight came. We had several despatch riders with us on brand new motorcycles, Ivory Calthorpes[1]. An order was passed along for all despatch riders to leave their bikes beside the road and ride on the tanks. Earlier we had driven across a little road over fields and I could see the Vimy memorial; it appeared to be damaged. Nearby was an overgrown little cemetery for German soldiers. It had iron crosses instead of stone ones and openwork like filigree, painted black but now all rusted.

We continued on through the day. Those huge horse-drawn carts always seemed to be in the way and, as in a traffic jam, the line of vehicles grew longer. All we had to eat were the good old army biscuits. The only stuff to drink was vino. We seemed to have plenty of that though I forget how we came by it. At one of those frustrating halts, we put a line of full bottles on a wall and shot them off with our revolvers. At another particularly long stop there was an ambulance in front of us. It was an army improvisation, being a small new metal-bodied

---

[1] *Launched In the late 1920s by the Minstrel & Rea Cycle Company. The design was sit-in as opposed to the traditional sit-on design.*

The Reservist 65

Dunkirk

"A colossal military disaster"

THOUSANDS OF Allied soldiers were evacuated from the beaches and harbour of Dunkirk between 26th May and 4th June 1940, after large numbers of Belgian, British, and French troops were cut off and surrounded by German troops around the mid-point of the six-week Battle of France. Winston Churchill called this "a colossal military disaster", saying "the whole root and core and brain of the British Army" had been stranded at Dunkirk and seemed about to perish or be captured. Their rescue was a "miracle of deliverance".

After the Phoney War of October 1939 to April 1940, Germany invaded Belgium, the Netherlands and France on 10 May 1940. Three of their panzer corps attacked through the Ardennes and drove northwest to the English Channel. By 21st May, German forces had trapped the British Expeditionary Force (BEF), the remains of the Belgian forces, and three French field armies, along the northern coast of France. Commander of the BEF, General Viscount Gort, saw evacuation across the Channel as the best course of action, and began planning a withdrawal to Dunkirk, the closest usable port.

Late on 23rd May a halt order was issued by the German army and it was left to the Luftwaffe to attempt to destroy the trapped BEF, French and Belgian armies until the order was rescinded on 26th May. This gave trapped Allied forces time to construct defensive works and pull back large numbers of troops to fight the Battle of Dunkirk.

On the first day 7,669 Allied soldiers were evacuated but by the end of the eighth day 338,226 of them had been rescued by a hastily assembled fleet of over 800 boats. Many troops were able to embark from the harbour's protective mole/breakwater onto 39 British Royal Navy destroyers, four Royal Canadian Navy destroyers and civilian merchant ships. Others waded from the beaches, waiting for hours in shoulder-deep water. Some were ferried to the larger ships by a flotilla of hundreds of merchant marine boats, fishing boats, pleasure craft, yachts and lifeboats from Britain. The BEF lost 68,000 soldiers during the French campaign and had to abandon most of its tanks, vehicles and equipment.

Dunkirk

van with no side windows in the body. It was painted like an ambulance and looked smart and clean. There was no driver but this was nothing out of the ordinary as generally when things moved on, the drivers returned.

We never dreamed the thing was in actual use. After all, an ambulance could have forced its way through. The sun was hot and so were the metal sides of the van. After two hours we decided to open the back. It had four dead men in it; one of them had no feet. We shut the doors; the smell was horrible. We stopped leaning on it after that.

Then suddenly we noticed that the officers had disappeared. It had happened silently and we were now on our own. We cursed them but, looking back, I realise that if anyone was to be saved, it had to be the officers first, else how could an army be rebuilt? At the time we thought what a lot of bastards they were. In fairness to some very brave men, I do not think they would have gone if they could have helped it. Then an order came down the column, where it came from no-one knew, but everyone was to make for Watteau.

I found that somehow I was now responsible for three tanks and two passenger despatch riders. I don't know how this came about nor where the rest got to, but with the traffic blocks and presumably other traffic coming from intersections, people and units got separated.

I think we reached Watteau the next day. It was

Dunkirk

supposed to be general HQ but when we arrived it was deserted. I looked round for sleeping quarters. We had been dive-bombed once, for the first time, and we had not found it very pleasant. I wanted the tanks under cover. I found the ideal place: a long high shed adjoining a big house. I had the tanks backed in, one in front of the other, and closed the doors. Then I went round the house. There were ten of us and no-one had slept for two or three days. I arranged a guard and allotted two men to each double bed. It was worked in such a way that no man would be woken out of turn. Meanwhile some of the men had found a sack of potatoes and we already had some tinned beef. They made a fire, put a big saucepan on it and were sitting round happily peeling spuds. I thought of the time when I had last peeled them. Unlike me these men were really happy tackling it. Attitudes had changed because of the German army.

And then we had an interruption. A British army captain walked in and said, "You will have to clear out of here, sergeant. My unit is coming and I have earmarked this place as the officers' mess." I asked him how he had got past my sentry and he laughed. I told him I was not shifting that night. For one thing I was first. Two, it was the best place for the tanks, and three, my men were very tired and I was not going to have them move the tanks that night. He told me I would have to move as he had already chalked OM on the door. I rubbed it off. My

Dunkirk

men stood up and looked nasty, and eventually he said he would try and find somewhere else.

I went out and told the sentry what I thought of him, then gave them all a lecture on fifth columnists and said that even now we had not seen this man's papers. And then I told them that he was not to be allowed back in again that night. I also reminded them where the tanks were. "If he comes back," I told them, "Shoot him."

I saw them all to bed like a good mother and went up to a single bed in a top room. I put my revolver under my pillow and did not undress.

Sometime in the night the same captain came into the room. He ordered me to leave the place and I was immediately out of bed and at him. I pushed him down the first short flight of stairs and stood half-way down with my gun aimed. "You are lucky I have young soldiers," I said, "Now get out." He went.

(I saw him back at the depot after Dunkirk. As I passed him I saluted, and until he spoke I did not know him. "Hallo sergeant," he said, "You got back all right then? Do you know if you are coming to my regiment?" I smiled and told him I did not think so, and thus we parted.)

We left Watteau the next day and we were not alone on the road. We caught up with other vehicles going the same way. Word drifted back that we were to make for Dunkirk. Later, word came again that all vehicles were to be left five miles outside the town. How these orders

The Reservist 69

Dunkirk

got through I do not know but that is how it was. We continued on until late afternoon when we reached the stationary tail of the dumped vehicles. The road was full of vehicles left two by two and, for the most part the road was on an embankment, one row of vehicles each side slewed round and pointed at the ditch. In some places it was a job to squeeze past.

As it got darker I saw a man I knew still sitting in the driving seat of his tank. In peacetime I had borrowed three shillings and sixpence *[17 pence]* from him. In all my army borrowing he was the only man I ever bilked *[withheld money from]*, and that was because we had been separated before pay day. I told him it was no good sitting in his tank and to hoof it for Dunkirk. As he climbed out, I told him I owed him money but could not pay that minute. So he let it run. I never saw him again and still owe it.

Some may wonder why the vehicles were not destroyed when abandoned. The first and simple answer is that no-one thought of it. The second answer is that few knew how to, as we could not blow them up. It would have been foolhardy to try to fire them with petrol. And the draining plugs were so hard to get at that if the other vehicles were all burning, with bullets going off at any angle, it would have been hazardous for the one doing the job and the men following could not have passed along the road. Imagine squeezing through miles of

Dunkirk

stationary traffic, all burning!

We still carried our equipment; the most important were the haversack and gas mask. The big packs had never been collected and I saw a big heap of them burning at the roadside as we left Arras. That is where my pyjamas and my chess set finished up. Our remaining haversacks were full of cigarettes and tobacco from the NAAFI. The gas mask had been slung as its case was much more useful without it.

As we walked, the way was lit first by a village burning on our right and later by one on our left. We arrived at a T junction and there was a military policeman standing as if on traffic duty. I do not know who gave him orders or what happened to him, but he was doing his job and he said if we went to the left we would come to Dunkirk, but it might be in enemy hands. If we went to the right we would come to Le Mans which, while not offering the opportunity of escape like Dunkirk, was still unoccupied. I chose the left and, as we parted, he warned us to be careful. I have often thought of that man. No-one was there to see whether he went as well. Back in England he could have easily said that he was overrun and nobody would have queried it. But he stood there doing his duty.

I have often taken the 'micky' out of the 'Redcaps'[1] but

---

[1] *'Redcaps' referred to members of the Royal Military Police (RMP) because of the scarlet covers on their peaked caps or scarlet coloured berets. The RMP is the corps of the British Army responsible for the policing of army service personnel.*

The Reservist 71

Dunkirk

I have seen them do some difficult jobs. (Two years later at Alamein the military police were in charge of traffic. It was necessary to have six additional tracks parallel with the single desert road and they named each of these tracks 'Sun', 'Moon', 'Hat', 'Ship' and so on, and each track was marked every ten yards with a pole stuck in the ground. Each pole had a cut-out shape on it of a sun, ship, or whatever, to show which track was which. These poles carried their signs right across our front, through our mines and then through Jerry's, to within 200 yards of Jerry's positions.)

So we turned left. We found the road was now clear of vehicles and we trod warily, walking on the grass verge. We saw a burning building by the roadside. It looked like a warehouse and as we neared it, we could hear military orders being given and the noise of arms drill. It was about four in the morning. We wondered who else could be doing this but the Germans?

We crept along on the other side of the hedge and saw that it was a company of our own guards, probably the same ones as from Arras. By the light of the burning building the sergeant major was giving them arms drill. We stood watching and after a few minutes he called the roll. We went on, but those guards did not retire. They formed part of the defensive ring around Dunkirk that allowed us to get away.

Then we reached the town. On the right of the first

Dunkirk

paved street was a damaged truck with several dead soldiers at its side. Men and truck had been burned. I was surprised to see that signs of the fire were only slight. The corpse nearest me looked deeply sunburned and his moustache and hair looked untouched. It must have been lack of air that had killed them. Farther down the road on the other side I saw a soldier who appeared to be asleep in a doorway in which he had sheltered. His head was missing.

We found our way through the apparently deserted place till we found the sea. Across the water what looked like an oil dump was on fire with thick, dense smoke billowing from it in two columns. On the sand was a long queue of men, all like us, unwashed, tin-hatted and tired. We joined the tail of the queue. The head of it was at a pier and at the end of the pier were two boats. I do not know how long we lined up, but I do not think it was more than two hours.

We saw two men try to take advantage of their warrant officer rank. They marched smartly along the beach as if on a message, and were halfway to the pier when they were stopped by two naval ratings who, after questioning them, sent them back to the end of the queue. Though by the way they were being looked at by other men in the queue, I do not think they would have made it in any case.

The pier itself was kept clear and once on it you could

The Reservist 73

Dunkirk

get on which boat you liked, if there was more than one. We had two to choose from. I suppose when a boat was full it sailed. The boats did not 'fit' the pier and it was about six feet up to the deck of the first one.

"Let's get on here, Sarge," said one of my blokes.

I said, "No, it's too high, let's get on this little yellow one." The smaller one was three feet down and I could fall onto that one. We got on and the same man said, "Let's lie on deck". It certainly was a lovely day with beautiful sunshine, but I thought that if we wanted to rest, we needed the shade, and said "No, we will go downstairs."

I had not slept for days and I had been issued with special pills to keep me awake if necessary but had not used them. We went below and I found some sacks; as soon as I lay down I was asleep. I knew when the boat was underway and later heard in my sleep shells from German guns hitting and exploding either on or near the boat. My same faithful follower woke me. He said "Sarge, they are shelling the boat." I said, "Well let them bloody well shell it then but leave me alone."

When we reached Dover some stretchers were disembarked first. Up to now I have not reported any hearsay in my account of the evacuation of Dunkirk, and I have left out anything I did not see myself. But there were some terrible things told to me by various, mostly younger, men and I decided that I would only report what

Dunkirk

I saw myself. At the time though, I saw that little boat fill up with men and saw no stretchers go aboard. I did see them taken off and my men told me that eight men had been killed on deck and 16 wounded. They also said that the bigger boat had been sunk. I can't be sure of any of it.

At Dover we were given a meal and put on a train. The Women's Voluntary Service walked along the carriages giving us each a bar of chocolate and ten Woodbines. We took the fags even though we still had the Arras ones; we could always give them away.

We arrived eventually at Alton. It was a pretty place and the next day we strolled about with our tin hats on the back of our heads to proclaim who we were. The next day we were sent back to the old depot[1] at Wool.

This did not seem very welcoming; they were at a loss to know what to do with us. The sergeant's mess was out of bounds – they could not have had room for this sudden influx – and we strolled about with our buttons undone and tin hats on the back of our heads. I was given a salutary lesson though. In the peacetime army there had been a provost sergeant in my unit who was very regimental. He had to be; that was his job. It was said that anywhere you touched him he could show you a scar; he had been in so many fights with drunks and other trouble makers. In the past he had fallen from a

[1] *Now the home of a tank museum.*

Dunkirk

station platform down amongst the train wheels and his troops had stuck their feet over the edge in an effort to keep him there. He had crawled out on the other side. When I knew him in peacetime he was also drum major and had once advertised for drummers. At the time I was fed up with tank driving and had answered the advertisement. But he did not have enough replies and when he went out on pension, the band was put in mothballs in the officers' mess.

And now I heard his familiar voice.

"Put your hat on straight! Do those buttons up!" There he was, as spick and span as a peacetime soldier with a pre-war uniform, all brass buttons and polish. He wore a sergeant's red sash, a cheese-cutter hat *[a cap with a broad, square brim]* and had a long cane under his arm. He also wore his old rank, four inverted chevrons at the bottom of each arm with a fife above. When a sergeant answered him back, saying, "You should have been there," *[in Dunkirk]* he said, "I left there after you, son. I got back this morning."

I shook hands with him, having first straightened myself up, and after a few minutes chat, asked him how he happened to re-acquire his old rank. He said he had joined the territorials while on pension, as a trooper again. The unit had no band and after a time he suggested to his colonel that his old unit might help. The outcome was that his old colonel presented his new colonel with a

Dunkirk

complete band and he was put in charge of it once more.

At the depot I was the only sergeant from my unit who had arrived. About 50 of the men had turned up and I took charge of them. I had to draw kit for them and sign for it all. You can get thousands of pounds worth of gear from the army for nothing. As long as you sign for it you can have it. I signed for a barrack room, complete with windows all checked and not broken or cracked. I signed for the beds the men were to sleep on, though it would have been difficult to steal them. I signed for the coir biscuits which served as a mattress, three for each bed. Brooms, mops, blankets, bolsters, coal buckets and fire appliances. I did not ever hand the stuff back again and maybe they are still holding me to it.

I could not get any leave as there was no-one to take over, but for the fortnight I was there I arranged for my wife to come down. We were able to get lodgings with a barrack warden who treated us very well and only charged one pound a week for both of us.

Sergeant Bill managed to wangle himself a week at home but they knew where he was and sent for him. He wrote a letter asking for leave and he was told he was to return to the depot. He then wired to ask if they meant 'now' and 36 hours later he was back.

While things were being sorted out they could not find much for us to do. If my wife had not been there I would have been fed up to the teeth but it was nearly as good

Dunkirk

as a leave after all.

My wife and I were strolling round the lanes surrounding the depot when we met big Frank from the old horse guards, the man who had lost his teeth over the side at St Nazaire.

I said, "Hello Frank, you got back all right then?"

"And I got my teeth," he said. At the time, not having false teeth myself, I had not thought much about that incident. To him, of course, it was all important. All that winter without proper teeth! How had he managed when there was nothing to eat but army biscuits? And despite all the jumble of the British Expeditionary Force coming back as they had, his teeth were at the depot awaiting him.

※ ※ ※

Rebuilding an army

AFTER ABOUT a fortnight our brigade had been sufficiently re-formed to be on its own once more. With its three regiments somewhere in the adjacent countryside, the brigade HQ – to which I still belonged – was moved to Greaseborough, a village just outside Rotherham, and for some reason known locally as 'soft water town'.

I had been allowed to escort my wife back to her home town of Middlesbrough, then to join the unit two days later, thereby missing the settling-in process.

I reached Greaseborough in the evening and reported to HQ in the village hall. I found out later that the whist drives and mothers' meetings were still being held there. To my surprise, there was no proper camp and I was given an address where I was to be billeted. The local people were doing their best for the army and really put themselves out to make us comfortable.

I was sent to the home of the coal mine secretary, a big house with a semi-circular drive at the front. I was asked whether I wanted my bath at night or in the morning, and was told I could leave my heavy army boots outside my door for the maid to clean. As my unit was now at full stretch, hurrying to get the men retrained, we were out on first drill parade at six in the morning. This billet did not suit me for several reasons: the early start was one, and

Rebuilding an army

I saw nothing to stop my wife from joining me if I could find a suitable place. The secretary and his wife were both good people and were upset that they were not being allowed to do their bit.

I explained to my sergeant major that I needed more suitable accommodation for my wife, and he gave me the address of a retired headmistress from the local school. She was a nice old lady and readily agreed to have my wife as well. She did hesitate when I mentioned the dog though. She said she had never had one before but was willing to try it. Her teenage son was delighted however, and my wife rejoined me. After two days the old lady, much to the astonishment of her erstwhile pupils, was to be seen taking the dog for a walk.

My early rising did not worry her either. Every morning, in spite of our protests, she brought us both tea in bed at 5.30 and left me some hot water for shaving. Every day there was a basket of fresh fruit in the hall for my wife and me to help ourselves when we wanted and, although she received the army allowance for my board, all she charged extra for my wife was 15 shillings a week. On the whole, I think both she and her son enjoyed the change.

I should have liked to have written to her after the war, but I hesitated. Did her son get involved in it? Would she still be alive? If one or the other had gone, then it might only upset the survivor to be reminded. I did not write.

Rebuilding an army

   Meanwhile, the unit had been equipped with little canvas-topped cars and vans which held six men and their weapons. We began taking trips around the countryside carrying out map reading and military exercises. These vehicles made an easier drive than the tanks they represented. We used to drive to a particular map reference, take up a defensive position, wait for the lieutenant to come round and criticise us, then go home again. At one of these halts the lieutenant taught me a new way to use bad language. I had quite a good vocabulary but when he said, "On your left things were all right but on your right, you have miles and miles of sweet f--- all", it sounded funny. I have forgotten his strategy but I remember his words.

   None of the men knew rifle drill. The only small arms they had ever handled was a revolver. We were issued with rifles and they were old ones at that. As an ex-infantry man I was familiar with rifles but I had not seen any as old as this before. If I could get hold of any now, I know I could make a few bob as they would be antiques. However, at the time it fell to me to show the lads how to use them and drill with them. Rifle drill consists of a lot of shouting by the instructor while the lads listen, then he has to do it himself to prove he is as good as he talks.

   There were two streets of houses very near the HQ, and separating the back gardens was a strip of smooth

The Reservist 81

Rebuilding an army

asphalt, ideal as a drill ground. The only problem was that I had to shout loudly to show the HQ that we were doing the job properly.

One lovely sunny morning, the men were lined up with their backs to the gardens on one side with me facing them as usual. They were standing 'at ease' with the rifles and were doing a lot less than I was when a woman came out from a house behind them.

"You bullying little devil", she said, "why don't you let them have a rest and a cup of tea?" She was still behind the men and on every face there was a huge grin, partly at my expense and partly because they really had been having an easy time. They could not do it as a drill movement yet, so I told them to do it on their bayonets. Then I gave the orders to slope arms, turn right and quick march. I marched them down the woman's garden path and, as she had not had time to close it, straight through the door into her kitchen. They were still 'on the slope' and the ceiling was only an inch away from their bayonets. I said, "Mark time", and with their heavy boots on they banged away for a bit. When I said to order arms they did it with precision, and 12 rifle butts went bang on the floor. Then I said, "Stand at ease" and there were two bangs: butts and boots.

The poor woman, who was pregnant, was in quite a panic by now and asked what I had brought them in for. I told her that it was her suggestion that they wanted

Rebuilding an army

a cup of tea and a rest. I looked at the men and they agreed. As tea was on ration she had to borrow some from her neighbour, but she did her duty. That night I took my wife down to meet her and her miner husband. My wife was embarrassed when, with us all present, our hostess espied a smart soldier walking past her front window.

"Boy!" she said, "I would like to wrap my legs round that!"

While we were retraining, the 'local defence volunteers' (which became the Home Guard) were forming, and they also had to be trained. They did not have rifles, just broomsticks, and some of our NCOs had to show them how to do the drill. The trouble was that the NCOs were in the same boat as the volunteers and it was assumed, wrongly, that they would know how to handle a rifle. At the same time the LDVs were made up of a large percentage of old-timers who did know the drill.

I was lucky enough not to be picked for this duty; it was evening work *[as many of the LDVs would have work during the day]* and involved not only an hour's drill but driving to another place to do it. I would have seen little of my wife as it would have meant being away mostly from six in the morning till eight at night. I was stung once, however. I was sent for by the major and told a tale. The previous night a young corporal had been sent to drill the LDVs but did not know how to do it. If he

Rebuilding an army

had told the major he knew nothing about it, I do not doubt that he would have been excused, but I suppose he thought he might endanger his stripes, and kept quiet. The LDVs took the mickey out of him rotten and, according to the major, he came back in tears. (He was not busted, the major realised the fault.) So the major approached me.

"I want you, sergeant, to go there tomorrow and give them a rough time. I want them paid back for what they did to that corporal."

As it happened, this was the local group and their parade was held on the sports field. They generally repaired to the clubhouse for a drink after the drill and, with the exception of the corporal episode, that was the way it usually ended for the day.

All that had been given to me as a young recruit, I gave them back that day. And halfway through I asked them if any of them wanted to take the micky out of me. Then I gave them a bit extra. It happened to be a Sunday and the wives and sweethearts were round the edge watching and, unbeknownst to me, my wife was amongst them. Before I dismissed the volunteers I told them it was a serious business and in future to come there to work not to show off. "So in future", I said, "don't bring your bloody women with you."

They went without attacking me but did not invite me for a drink. As I left, my wife came up to me and told me that when I had given the men that final admonishment, the woman next to her turned and said, "Who does that little black bastard think he is!" That made my day. We did not drill them any more after that.

We put in long hours at Greaseborough but the time passed enjoyably enough. It was lovely weather. I had my wife with me, and the contrast with our billets in France was fantastic.

The orderly room in the village hall had to cope with some small difficulties. One man was doing a week's detention and, like my own 14 days in Bethune, there was nowhere other than the HQ for him to go. Pay day was also the day for the mothers' meeting and because of lack of space the prisoner was temporarily released. He quickly saw his chance, joined the pay queue and received the usual one pound. Before anyone realised it, he was on the local bus to the town and naturally was not 'found' till he came back in the evening.

My mate from promotion time, Sergeant Bill, happened to be billeted next door to me and had started walking out with his landlady's teenage daughter. I knew he was married and had two little girls, and one day my own landlady asked me point blank for the truth about him. Was he married? The people next door were her friends and he was talking of an engagement. I did not admire his conduct so I told her; everyone had made us welcome and had given us their trust.

Rebuilding an army

The rest of the country was suffering under the Blitz and I had seen Sheffield[1], but it had never reached near enough to us for the unit to help, or maybe we had too much training to do.

The unit moved on, this time to Keele Hall[2] near Newcastle under Lyme. The wives went home and we reverted to a normal routine. As the HQ of the brigade, we were billeted in the hall itself, while the three regiments of the unit were stationed in three concentric rings in the grounds; this meant we passed three guard rooms going out and were challenged by three lots of sentries on returning.

The old hall was a curious place. It had no roof over the centre but we found enough cover at the sides. The library was denuded of books and that left the fitted bookcases empty, except for one narrow case in a corner. This appeared to be filled with leather-bound volumes from floor to ceiling. On investigation we found the 'books' were false fronts and the whole of this section was a narrow 'secret' door. When a button was pressed the door opened, revealing a stairway no wider than 18 inches. This went up, without any other exit, to the second floor, where a second door opened into what

---

[1] *Sheffield was bombed on the evening of December 12th 1940, when hundreds were killed.*

[2] *Keele Hall is a 19th-century mansion house and Grade II listed building.*

must have been the maid's bedroom. What a lovely life to have the money to put your thoughts into realities! There were similar signs of this man's inclinations in the bas-relief plaster frescoes on the main staircase and ceiling centre pieces. Let us hope he had value for his efforts. There was some beautiful pornography.

While at Keele I heard news of the corporal with whom I had had blows, and who was instrumental in my 14 days field punishment. In France he had been promoted to sergeant and officers' mess caterer. This used to be one of the biggest 'fiddles' open to other ranks, and he had tripped up. He was now a private. One day, while I was walking in Newcastle under Lyme, we saw each other. He crossed the road. So did I. We came face to face. Calling him by his surname I congratulated him on getting through Dunkirk and asked if he was getting along all right. He stood to attention and called me 'sergeant'. I told him I was pleased to have met him and went on. He could take it how he liked.

One night I went out with Sergeant Bill and his corporal mate. We were supposed to be in by 10.30pm, but had had a few drinks and it was nearer midnight as we arrived home. Sergeant Bill was really worried about our reception at this hour, and I told him we were sergeants and would get in OK, but he kept on about it. There were three different lots of sentries to pass and they did not know us. The corporal had had enough to drink and was singing happily to himself, not a care in the world. He had linked arms with both of us so was able get along. Sergeant Bill suddenly had an idea.

"Look how bad he is," he said. "Let's pinch him for being drunk and say we are late because of the job we have had getting him home." This was his "mucking-in mate", the man who had been promoted at the same time. I said, "Leave it to me", and as we were challenged I answered in my best parade ground voice, "Brigade HQ." Each sentry had brought his bayonet down in the regulation manner, and each returned it on hearing the magic words, but it makes you wonder who your friends are doesn't it?

Shortly after this Sergeant Bill and I were posted to the 50th Tank Regiment. The cavalry men still did not like tank men and we did not like them, so both sides were suited. Bill lost his mate and I wondered if they would miss each other. The posting was made on a Saturday and the sergeant major made sure we travelled with no money on us. He stopped us our sergeants' mess fees for this and that, and we were left with nothing (there was no credit as you might get killed the next day; all army pay and rations are computed with this contingency in mind).

So we went out broke, on a Saturday, with no pay till next Friday and no smokes; and how could we borrow in a strange unit? We would not even know who to approach. We were sent to Pocklington near York, and arrived too late for dinner. The RSM was a man I had known in the peacetime army when he was a sergeant nearing retirement; he now had a new lease of life. He would not be sent abroad, he was too old for that, but he was a good soldier and he would have gone if they had let him. He was doing his bit by using his experience to help younger men.

He ignored the new battle dress and walked around resplendent in the 'superfine' uniform complete with a Sam Browne[1] of the pre-war army. He knew me well. I had been the private he used to pick on for little jobs. Years earlier we had once paraded to sweep the snow from a football pitch, and I was secretly instructed not to take a broom with me, but to bring one back. Another time, just before a general's inspection, 'B' Company had put a foot high single wire fence round their flower bed and I was the one given the pliers to thieve the wire for our own lawn.

He told us that we had come to the wrong unit, but that as we were broke we were free to have our meals in the mess till he could send us on our way. In the meantime he showed us round the camp. We came to a canal with a little humped back bridge. He paused here and told us the brigadier had made all the men jump in dressed in full

[1] *The Sam Browne is a wide belt, usually leather, supported by a narrower strap passing diagonally over the right shoulder.*

kit, and then swim across.

"Officers and all?" I asked.

"The lot," he said, "Colonel and all."

"Did you go in Bert?" He looked really shocked. He had a bit of weight on now – as well as his lovely suit.

"I went over the bridge," he said. I think even if the brigadier had given him a direct order he would have stared him out.

Later that night he told us the unit we wanted was in Llantrisant[1] in Wales, and that we were to go on Sunday morning. I was glad I had met old Bert.

The next morning we were on our way. At York we saw the rail transport officer and got a free meal in the rail buffet. We did this again on reaching London.

Bill had a wife and two daughters in Enfield, and by hanging about a bit we were able to deliberately miss the last train that day to Wales. Bill inveigled the rail transport officer (who happened to also be a corporal) into sending a truck round the side of the station to pick us up and take us to Enfield, and Bill enjoyed a reunion with his family. We both had tea and his wife had enough money to buy us some smokes.

We left in the morning, not too early, and as we were travelling towards our destination we could go by train using our warrants. We had dinner courtesy of the rail

[1] *Llantrisant is a town in the county borough of Rhondda Cynon Taf in Glamorgan, about 12 miles north west of Cardiff.*

transport officer at Paddington, and he told us we could get a casual payment from the rail transport officer at Victoria. We travelled there (for free) and received ten bob each. We bought some fags and accepted another meal from the rail transport officer at Paddington, as we had such a long journey in front of us. When we arrived at Llantrisant we had to ask the rail transport officer there to phone the unit for transport, and eventually arrived at a canvas camp in the evening.

At the field gate we were shocked to see one of our oldest pre-war tanks, but it was a false alarm. They had no tanks at all *[presumably no working tanks - Ed]*.

I was soon in trouble here. As new arrivals we checked in at the guard tent and enquired of the guard commander about sleeping quarters and where to draw blankets. And It was now about eight o'clock and we had had nothing to eat since midday. He told us everybody was at a concert in the NAAFI marquee and we would get nothing till the concert was over. So we went to the concert, stumbled over chairs in the darkness, found two empty ones and sat down. They were two placed in front of the RSM but we took them in our ignorance. (Later I guessed they may have been left vacant to give the RSM a better view.)

There were six elderly women on stage, dressed in national costume and singing 'Men of Harlech'. I had heard it before and passed the time making caustic

Rebuilding an army

comments. Someone behind me told me to keep quiet or else I would be in the guard 'house' for the night. I took exception to his high-handed manner and answered in like terms. I was suddenly surrounded by two men and conducted to the rear of the tent, where I was confronted by the owner of the voice. It was the great man himself. He naturally would know the voices of all his sergeants and was as surprised as I was. However, he did us a good turn really, as he sent men with us to get a meal and accommodation.

The army is very logical and the conclusions it arrives at can generally be foreseen some way ahead. Naturally neither Bill nor I had ever acted as orderly sergeant at this place before, therefore it must be our turn. As only one was needed each week, I guessed it was my turn now. It would probably be Bill's turn to be guard commander.

The orderly sergeant's duties are the most onerous and sustained of any there can be when not actually in the firing line. The man doing the job has to be up and ready for inspection by reveille[1] to see that every other person is on his feet by then. He also has to be on parade as smartly turned out as ever at 'Last Post' at ten at night, and see all lights are out at 10.15pm. Then, still on duty,

[1] *Reveille is a signal sounded from a drum or bugle to awaken military personnel and alert them for assembly, usually at sunrise.*

Rebuilding an army

he must go the sergeants' mess and be on hand till the RSM tells the caterer to close up, generally at 11 o'clock. In addition he has all manner of little duties to pass the time in between. I was quite right. I was orderly sergeant and Bill was guard commander.

I soon came unstuck; I had been in six different units by this time and each had its own little foibles. The pet one here was that any accused men summoned for trial by their squadron leader had to be found and herded to the office at the time laid down. In all the other units I'd known the accused was just warned to be there and it was left to him. The usual thing was for the NCO to say, "OK, same place, same time," and that was that. Here, the names of any accused were given in to the office where the orderly sergeant collected them. The following morning he went round fetching the accused from their various duties and conducting them to where the trial was taking place. I knew nothing of this and on Tuesday, my first morning, there was a hue and cry for me. Where was the accused man? I did not know. The major was furious and I became an accused as well, charged with 'neglect of duty'.

Parading myself, I went before the colonel the next day. To my surprise he said there was no excuse for, as a senior NCO, I should have known the procedure, and I was 'severely reprimanded'. Next to being stripped of rank, this is the heaviest punishment I could be given and the most the commanding officer could do without a court martial. It would have stopped me going on any planned trips for three months, but more important it stopped any leave for the same period. I told the CO I would go for a court martial. He said as he had sentenced me all I could do was to make a general complaint, and I said I would.

During the war there were three men who did me ill turns. I am not of a nature to try to 'get my own back'. That seems a waste of time and I would find it too much bother to go through life totting up and memorising grudges in case whoever was concerned crossed my path again. The first of these ill turns was by the corporal in France and, with no help from me, he lost out.

Now I come to the second. Some days after the colonel's reprimand I was called into the adjutant's tent where I met the sergeant who had handed the job of orderly sergeant to me. The 'order board' in there had a typed list on it of all the duties that had to be carried out by the orderly sergeant during his tour. Now, newly added at the bottom was an order embracing the job I had not carried out. The adjutant explained the procedure, said both the sergeant and I had to give evidence on oath and, producing a Bible, administered the oath to each of us. He then asked me whether I had read the order board when I took over. I said I had, but pointed out that the last item was freshly added. He agreed and said he had

Rebuilding an army

to find out whether I had actually been told about it. He then asked the other sergeant, "Did you or did you not tell him?"

He replied, "Well sir, I don't like this. If I say 'No' I offend the sergeant major and if I say 'Yes' I offend the sergeant here." The adjutant said, "Sergeant, **you are on oath**."

The man looked at us both, paused a minute, and then said, "Well, yes." The adjutant could see it was an obvious lie. He looked at me, shrugged his shoulders, raised his eyebrows and snapped the Bible shut. He asked me what I wished to do and I told him I would drop it.

The adjutant must have talked about it in the mess. Three months later I left that unit, and a month after that I heard the sergeant was given the option of reverting to the ranks himself or being reverted for inefficiency. He threw his stripes in himself.

We moved on to Liverpool this time and I was immediately sent to hospital. I had varicose veins – an ongoing problem – and was ordered to Ormskirk for treatment, which involved an operation on each leg which, 30 years later, have proved no use at all. I was in for about two weeks and on release I learned that the unit had moved on again, this time to Whitby.

Once again red tape helped me. Some people seem to consider red tape a hindrance to the sweet running of things but it can be a help to men with initiative.

I have mentioned that the army runs on a day-to-day basis. Just think what a mess-up would occur for the pay office back home if a million men had been paid a month in advance and the enemy then dropped an atom bomb on them. All that money! Who could be blamed? The food is worked out in the same way. When I was at the hospital, my day's rations had been credited to the hospital and the rules did not permit my discharge until I had eaten the best part of my day's portion. Consequently, I could not be let out until two o'clock and I suppose they considered that I had enough food inside me to sustain me till I arrived in Whitby.

By the time I had reached Liverpool on the suburban line and found the main line station, I realised there was no way I could get to Whitby that day. It was suggested I could change at York, proceed to Scarborough and wait there on the platform for the milk train in the morning. My wife was in Middlesbrough, so I stayed on the train at York and got off at Darlington. My ticket was inspected and I was told I had made a mistake and would have to cross the line at Darlington and get back to York. However, I had done the Darlington to Middlesbrough run from Catterick many times during my courting days and knew that I could walk from the main line to the side line for Middlesbrough, avoiding all ticket barriers.

I arrived at Middlesbrough in the late evening and

asked the man selling tickets if there was anywhere I could stay on the station till the first train was due for Whitby. He looked horrified and suggested I go and find a YMCA or similar, and come back in the morning. I thanked him and went to my wife's home *[where she was staying with her mother]* for the night. She asked me when I would be leaving (people always ask this as soon as a soldier arrives), and I told her I would take the ten o'clock bus in the morning; the bus journey took two hours so this would easily get me to Whitby in time for dinner.

   I enjoyed that stolen night but it was no good telling the army that. If you tell or act a lie it has to be backed up. The regiment was billeted in a hotel on the seafront and as soon as I had finished my midday meal, I went to make a complaint.

   I told a sympathetic major that, having been discharged from hospital with a recommendation for ten days sick leave to give my legs a chance to recover, I had been sent out (with all that weight of kit) at a time which was too late to do the journey in one day. And, apart from the strain, it had cost me money for food and lodgings. The major agreed that it had been ridiculous and tried to make it up. I actually got board and lodging allowance and was paid for the ten days leave from the next morning, and allowed to go straight away. I was back in Middlesbrough for tea. And that levelled up with the 'severe reprimand'.

Ten days leave and then back to work. The regiment was all under the same roof; they had no vehicles yet but did have tank-type guns and small arms. As my role as a sergeant was normally to teach driving, there was not much I was wanted for. The lads were learning the theory of gunnery as well as wireless. So I was given the disgusting chore of sergeants' mess caterer. I had to run a bar and keep the drink account, which had to be checked by the RSM every morning. This was a boring job but I took an interest in the games room.

I prevailed on the captain in charge to buy a dozen chess sets, and I started a club. I wrote down some details and pinned it to the notice board, and in a short time had quite a few members, all entirely new to the game. I taught whoever wanted to learn and after a month had two 'ladders' going: one for novices and one for the rest. It was quite a success but in a way it led to my getting reduced to the ranks and moved to another unit.

The captain who had bought the chess sets (out of regimental funds) was a Scot and I do not think he liked to see money wasted. I had more duties thrust upon me and eventually found I could not do everything. The chess club was on its feet with 20 or so members and there were those who could teach the others so I felt able to give it up. It was not that I was fed up with it, I just did

Rebuilding an army

not have the time except for an occasional visit. But the Scot thought it was money down the drain. He would not see that I had other work taking up my time as the unit built up.

I was still caterer though, and every morning the RSM sent a man to clean up the place. One morning the chosen man was a member of my chess club, and a recruit at that. He was a public schoolboy, could play chess as well as I could and became a good friend; a friendship that survived the war years till his death in about 1965. He was always Stan to me.

When he reported back to me that first morning, I outlined his duties and told him that when he had done them he should be easily finished for the day by 10.30am. I added that when he left, he should keep out of everyone's way or else he would be caught for something extra. He reported to me at about the time I had said and seemed surprised that I did not inspect his work but let him go.

He served longer than I did in the war zone, and after the war he told me that he ended up as a major and tank squadron leader.

(It's queer, isn't it? From my account of things you would think me one of those hard-bitten cocky know-all barrack room lawyer types and maybe I am, but instead of typing happily away for the next two hours as I had intended, recalling Stan has upset things and I cannot carry on tonight.)

As Whitby was so close to Middlesbrough, I could see my wife now and then if I could get a relief at the bar. But Christmas was approaching and there was no prospect of any leave. I discovered that the sergeants' mess would be closed at four o'clock on Christmas Day and, unlike London buses, the normal bus service would be maintained. I was able to get away in time to catch the four o'clock bus, enjoy a few hours of a civilian Christmas, catch the ten o'clock bus and be back to my bar by midnight.

When I arrived the door to the place had been broken open and the place was in uproar. It was full of people and two men from the officers' mess were serving all the drink I had carefully checked. I asked them what was the meaning of it, noting that they were charging ten bob *[10 shillings/50 pence]* for a pint to anyone too drunk to realise it. They told me the RSM had invited the officers in and broken the place open himself. I asked how they were checking the sales and the spokesman pointed to a recess full of empty bottles; all they had to do was count them when they'd finished. I told them that, as they seemed to be doing all right, to put a couple of dozen extra there and we would all have a pound from the till. I took no part in the proceedings and had to wait till the end before I could go to bed, on the floor behind the bar. In the morning I had to leave it open to go for breakfast but that was not my worry now.

The RSM showed up mid-morning for the ritual check. This included 'dipping' the beer barrel and measuring all the opened spirit bottles. The barrel was measured with a four-sided dip-stick and, according to which size it was, there was a side of dip-stick to read. Doing this taught me the word 'firkin' as a size, and also that I was allowed all the whisky in the bottle neck for 'spills'. At a shilling *[5 pence]* a nip this gave me three shillings buckshee on each bottle sold.

But on this occasion I let the RSM do all the checking himself and he informed me that 'we' were about a fiver down. He looked at me as if he expected me to pay it, but I laughed tactfully. I presume it was just written off.

I was at Middlesbrough for New Year's Eve; I forget how that came about but I was bussing back to Whitby in the early morning of the first of January. In the sunrise the sky was red all over, so much so that it stuck in my mind, and made me think of the war that was still to come. I took it as a sign of a bloody year and I was right.

Shortly after Christmas someone wrote a eulogy in the Daily Mail to 'The men of the beret brigade'. It was pinned to the notice board for all to read. When I read it, the words, "the stern-eyed keen-faced resolute chins of the men' filled me up. It was hardly six months since we had been ordered to wear those stupid side hats. I wrote "all balls" on the notice and signed it.

Rebuilding an army

Two hours later the Scot captain found me. He was in a flaming temper and his brogue was making him stutter. Waving the notice at me, he asked if that was my signature. I said light-heartedly that it was and he put me under close arrest. It happened to be Saturday and I was due to go to Middlesbrough on Sunday. Like a fool, I told him this and asked if he could not manage open arrest. Naturally he said no, so on Sunday after church parade I caught the bus for Middlesbrough anyway.

On my return I was put under the escort of another sergeant. On Monday morning I saw the colonel. He said the first charge was a lot of rubbish but on the second one, as I was a senior NCO he was bound to give me a court martial. Well, I had not had one yet and I aimed to be a complete soldier. I think it punished my escort *[who had to accompany him until the court martial]* more than me. He had committed no crime but we always had to be together. He told me he never wanted to see me again.

I still had a further spell at home though, when my mother-in-law was taken ill. The army does its best and they gave me 48 hours leave, and as I could not be paid, the adjutant lent me a pound to go with. I was 'released from close arrest without prejudice to re-arrest', and arrived at the front door as the vicar was leaving, having given the last rites.

Yorkshire people have a very homely custom when a person is dying. They get the expiring one out of bed,

Rebuilding an army

take the bed downstairs and re-erect it in the front room, then they get the expiree down and into the bed again. The reason is that a corpse or coffin is too awkward to negotiate a small staircase. To my mind this custom means the patient knows his time has come, and this was the position with my mother-in-law. She was a hot-tempered woman and when I told her how lazy she was and how much trouble she was causing, she got in such a temper that she lived long enough to see the peace come and then for some years after.

I had to go back the next evening as the court martial was the following day at Scarborough. We had a blizzard which was so bad that the bus driver gave up at the Cross Keys inn just outside Middlesbrough. I sat there thinking for a minute, which left only one old lady and me on board. The inn was 100 yards away and the old lady only had a thin coat on. As she got off, there came a blast so cold it went through my army coat. She fainted and I carried her there.

This inn was known to me from my courting days. My wife-to-be had a very healthy appetite and if you went upstairs and paid one shilling *[5 pence]*, you could eat as much as you liked from a long table filled with all the food you could think of. If you ate everything in front of you and were still hungry, you changed chairs. Now 'there was a war on' and that was only a memory. However in the bar there was a reminder of the old days:

Rebuilding an army

a picture of a black boy. If a penny was inserted in a slot in the frame, the boy would roll his eyes continually for a minute. He appeared to be looking straight at you, and I endured this all night. There was no other amusement for a room full of people with no place to sleep and they all had pennies. I did manage to phone through to the RSM to explain where I was.

In the morning my escort and I walked across some fields and flagged down a train. On our arrival at the RSM's hotel he beamed with relief.

"Thank God you made it". (For how can you have a court martial without the prisoner?) He told me to go and have a quick shave and as I moved from the staircase he roared to me to stop and wait for my escort. I was under close arrest again. An hour later a three car entourage started for Scarborough. I told the RSM that we would not get through.

He said, "You are the prisoner," in such a way that it meant I was less than nothing. I had thought I was the most important thing they were taking, but let it pass.

The cars were open 'staff cars' and we travelled along so smoothly on the nice clear road that the RSM managed to look back at me in the second vehicle and give me a superior look. Then we caught up with the snow plough. There were six feet of snow in front of it and four feet each side. The RSM was furious and tried to bully the old Yorkshire men who made up the snow plough team. They told him they might meet the plough from Scarborough that day but probably not. It is a tricky job turning vehicles round in a road the width of a snow plough, but we managed it, returned to Whitby and took the next train.

The trial took place; there was nothing I could say and did not try. With an NCO there is no ceremony such as one reads about at officers' trials: no swords pointing towards the accused. He is just marched out and learns some days later in front of his colonel what the sentence is. This is because the court's findings are sent to the brigadier who can modify or presumably increase the punishment. In my case I was reduced to the ranks and transferred to another unit. I think the reason for the transfer is to safeguard the accused from any revenge from grudge-holders once he has lost the protection of rank. What surprised me was that while the provost sergeant was stripping the chevrons from my arms, the RSM was standing there crying. It had not been any of his doing and before I left the regiment he came up to me on the quiet (it would not have done to be seen) and shook hands, saying he was sorry about it all and wished me the best of luck in my new unit.

He was another old-timer doing his job. He had a glass eye and would not be going overseas, and probably could have kept out of it altogether if he had wished to.

The new unit, a sister regiment of the one I had just left,

was based in another hotel.

The continual changing from one unit to another means one gets used to making and losing friends very quickly. I have known men who have been bosom pals for months, even sharing a toothbrush, become separated by the width of one barrack room, then hardly ever pass the time of day with each other again. I had left one group of friends, some of whom I had known in peacetime. One sergeant major had actually been the corporal who had taught me to drive a tank, then had to start again.

However, there was a big welcome for me at the new unit. I had to take my meals in the dining hall and felt a bit queer going in amongst the troops once more. The first time was for tea; they were having a wonderful time with a glorious spread plus platefuls of cigarettes and beer (for tea). The sergeants were acting as waiters. I was beginning to think that they had either laid it all on just for me, or that it was like this every day, when someone told me that it was St David's day which the regiment always celebrated as a holiday. They were a Liverpool-Welsh regiment.

Later the colonel gave a little talk, then they started singing. The song was a hymn and it was only years later that I found out the words were not the right ones. They sang, "Bread of Heaven, feed me till I can eat no more[1]."

[1] *The correct words are "Bread of Heaven, feed me till I want no more".*

Rebuilding an army

This hymn was always sung on these little regimental get-togethers when there was always a special kind of atmosphere, but the words never varied.

This was the mob I was with through the rest of the war. They were a Territorial unit and things struck me as a bit funny at first. My favourite sergeant major was a little man, very smart and very regimental. I met him for the first time on the evening of that first day. I was playing a game of pontoon in a barrack room and in he walked, accompanied by a sergeant. My first thought was, it's my first day and I'm going to get done for gambling and, as I am a busted sergeant, one of the oldest men here and a senior soldier, they will say that I led the others astray.

However, the sergeant major sat down at the table, brought out his small change and took a hand in the game. He played well and after 20 minutes he was well in pocket. Then his style of play changed and he soon lost what he had won, possibly a bit more, and then he packed up. His attitude was that he would not take money off the lads. He was a different man on parade and would often hold one especially to read out some new order to us.

In the army, especially in peacetime, the top brass must surely know that in the general run of things the men have not had much education, yet the orders include some of the longest words in the dictionary. I soon realised that the sergeant major, although he

Rebuilding an army

understood these long words, could not read them, and usually someone nearby would say the word for him. I also noticed that while he would greet a man with, "Good morning, trooper", the trooper would answer, "Good morning Blank", calling him by his nickname. This did not quite add up, and I asked a newfound friend about it. He told me that as the regiment was Territorial, our squadron had all come from one factory and our present squadron leader had been the governor. When the unit was called to active service, he had called them all into the factory yard, told them what they had trained for had come to pass and then got them all to say the Lord's Prayer. The sergeant major, who had been an old soldier, had been the factory doorman. Most of these chaps had been the 'white collar' men and neither he nor they had got out of old habits. It was the same with the gambling, which is usually one of the most serious crimes in the army. Everybody did it, right through the ranks. Why should he pick on the lads?

This sergeant major was one of the genuine soldiers of the war. He was too short ever to be a tank commander and, hoping he would excuse my saying so, he could never have mastered the complications of the job. There were three different radios to control, the driver to direct and the gunner to control. He needed to know how to 'bracket his fire', which shells to use and what ground his tank could traverse, all at the same time. But he did try.

Rebuilding an army

Some men of his rank used the knowledge to keep at the back; he used his to try to get to the front.

(At Alamein, a replacement tank would arrive complete with crew, and once one of these appeared with old sergeant major Blank just peeping over the top; he could not get any higher. His major said, "Right, sergeant major, you have got here and seen it, now back you go," and the crestfallen sergeant major went back to base. That major and the two others of the three fighting squadrons were killed in that action, but more of that later.)

On the second day of my service with the 46th Tank Regiment I was called in front of the captain, second in command of my squadron. He was a man I had served under a long time before and had been one of the judges at the court martial so knew all about me. He gave me the choice of which section I served in but suggested the technical stores. He told me the corporal in charge was over active service age, and that when we went abroad I would take over. But I preferred to stay at 'duty'. One reason was that I hate office work; another was that there was only one technical corporal and he was always on call, and I would prefer to get away sometimes. I had seen that they were being issued with scout cars which I had had some experience with and told him I would like to go to them instead.

So I joined the scout cars as a driver. I was not very popular and, along with a lot of others who had been

Rebuilding an army

to France, was often called "Dunkirk Joe". This did not worry me; they were just trying to get back at an erstwhile sergeant. I knew more than they did about the cars and was soon explaining the numerous mechanisms involved. Naturally I was given the rough jobs.

The first of these was to proceed to a flat heath and introduce the sergeants to the car. This heath had an 'anti-picnic' trench *[to stop civilian cars crossing]* dug about four feet deep parallel with the road. I instructed the sergeants to take turns; most of them were keen to handle the car and listened to what I told them, but there was one cocky one. He went his own way and side-slipped into the trench when we were doing 40mph.

There was a rumour that if these flat topped vehicles turned over the occupants would be decapitated. During my long experience with them I have never known it to happen but the thought came to me at this time. We were travelling at 40mph on the two nearside wheels like a bicycle, and then my driver lost his nerve.

"What do we do now?" he asked. I told him to prepare to swing right, and to do it quickly when I told him. I then watched the bank for a break and when I saw a small one gave him the word. A quick wrench of the wheel and we were out. I met that man after the war at a horse fair in Yorkshire. He did not go abroad with us as he went for a commission *[presumably involving training in the UK]*.

My next assignment was to drive the colonel on a

Rebuilding an army

mapping tour of the area. We had two lieutenant colonels at the time and this one was the second in command (although later on was the man in charge). He was efficient and strict and no-one was anxious to drive him, so "Dunkirk Joe" got the job. It had rained heavily and the track the colonel directed me to take was water-logged. He sat beside me in the open vehicle marking his map. I stopped at an extra deep pool and suggested he got out. He asked why and I told him I would have to rush this one and the water would come over the top and drown him and his map. He got out and watched and when he saw the quantity of water that fell on his seat I was in line for promotion. That opportunity came up three months later.

The colonel had my squadron on parade and was reading out promotions and appointments. He read me out as lance corporal. My captain (the one at the court martial), said, "Excuse me sir, I only put down 'acting unpaid'". The colonel replied, "lance corporal". And I had my foot on the first rung of the ladder once more.

Before this elevation in rank the regiment had moved into Ashdown Forest, still under the senior colonel. This man was a martinet of the 14-18 war. He also had only one eye. The regiment could have gone into barracks at Maresfield but he would not have that.

"I will have camp in the forest," he said. And we did. The forest was thick with leaves from when William I had the place planted. We swept them up and this took place from 8am until 4pm. All leave was stopped and if the men wanted a woman they could find one locally. And there was no smoking in working hours. The result was that the officers as well as the men were going for a quick smoke when they could. The padre and the medical officer were dead against this whole procedure and whenever possible the medical officer sent the lads on sick leave.

The colonel decided that his tent was to be pitched where there was a big ant hill. This was removed and a line of oil was poured daily around the perimeter of the colonel's tent to stop the ants returning.

Now the colonel transferred his efforts to the road outside the camp. He did not like the high speeds of the drivers using it. He procured big oil drums, had them painted white then placed on each side of the road in such a way that it was awkward for vehicles to pass even when approaching each other. He also placed regimental police on the road with instructions to order vehicles to keep down to 4mph. He would drive out himself though, and return right up to his tent at 30mph or more.

The colonel's own staff driver went to hospital with migraine brought on by practically impossible orders. Driving across country he would go through a field gate and perhaps steer for the exit gate at a diagonal. That method was stopped. He was told to drive at top speed straight for the hedge and, on command, swing suddenly right or left. I wrote a 'poem' about him. I got the orderly room clerk to type it out for me and he typed out several copies which, without my knowledge, he distributed to various strategic people. This meant that the 'poem' went all round the regiment. Here it is:

Now listen to the tale of our colonel,
The man who would never give in;
Whose single-eyed purpose shines brightly,
(Though he started in life as a quin).

A man who through life fought on bravely,
In a war where no other had hope,
A war whose strong basic foundations,
Were built up on blanco and soap.

The others all finished in '18
After four years of battle and strife,
But our colonel give in? No, not likely,
He took on a club chair for life.

Here he laid down the laws of the army,
With much vim and vigour and wit,
Till before he could drive them all balmy,
They let him come back for his 'bit'.

Now he lives in a tent in the woods sir,
Where he thinks about Poonah and soap,
And we for our part all think about him,
And the trees and a good piece of rope.

We have swept up the woods now a treat sir,

Rebuilding an army

We have scrubbed all the trees free from bark,
We work at it all the weekends sir,
And then we get up with the lark.

But we thank God for just two small mercies,
And without them our lives would be hell,
Firstly, leaves do not fall in the summer,
And next, he has one eye unwell.

Shortly after writing this I was sent on a short course for about ten days to learn about mines, explosives and booby traps, and when I returned the colonel had gone. He had tried to use his tank driver in the same way as he had used the car driver. The tank driver was told not to use his own eyes but rely on orders. At good speed he drove straight down a six feet drop. He knew it was coming but the colonel had said nothing. The lid of the cupola became released from its holding and crashed shut, smashing some of the colonel's fingers.

He never came back to the unit after his stay in hospital. The second in command did not replace him though. A more senior man came and was placed above him, and it was not until he was wounded at Alamein that command went to the man who gave me my first stripe.

Things now became normal again and we reverted to being soldiers. Leave started again, the men were happier, and we got back to training.

Leave was the topmost thought in the minds of

everyone. We were all supposed to get ten days every three months but, owing to sudden cancellations, the interval could be much longer. There were all different kinds of leave too: sick, survivors, compassionate and so on. The trouble was that if any person on the same list as you got a different type of leave from normal, he just jumped the queue and everyone else went down a turn. Then all leave would be stopped by someone above and it was hard to explain to wives at home why your own leave had been deferred again. To them it always seemed that the man next door was at home but not you; was there another woman somewhere? Women think like that and the only answer is to be there.

One day I posted a letter to my wife telling her I would be home the next day. The post box was outside the squadron office. The sergeant major and the quartermaster sergeant were both outside the office and saw me post the letter. It was about six at night. The sergeant major asked, "Is that to tell the wife you are on leave tomorrow?" When I said it was, he laughed and said, "Well, all leave is cancelled." I told him he might have informed me before I put the letter in the box, but he had no sympathy. He told me that the quartermaster sergeant was due to go on leave as well and his was also cancelled.

Just then a runner came from the orderly room and told the sergeant major that the colonel wanted to see lance

Rebuilding an army

corporal Harmer. "There he is," said the sergeant major. "Go on Harmer, see the colonel and maybe you will get your leave while you're there." He laughed heartily at his joke and off I went, wondering what the commanding officer had singled me out for.

He came straight to the point: he wanted to make me a sergeant but first he wanted to know what the court martial had been for. When I explained he said I would need a new background to build on. He would promote me to full corporal then send me on a tank instructors' course which would take three months. If I came back a Class One instructor he would then give me the third stripe (this was the same second-in-command who had made me lance corporal).

I listened with mixed feelings. It is often the present that is a priority in one's mind and this would mean goodbye to any leave for at least another three months. Then he gave me a ray of hope. "The course does not start for another fortnight," he said, "so that gives you time to go over the tanks in your own time, revising your knowledge of them."

The tanks had not altered much from my old peacetime ones; I knew them as well as I ever would and told him so. I also told him I was due for leave that day, and as it seemed there would be no chance of it for at least three months, could I not go anyway. I assured him I would get the Class One. He thought it a good idea and became

Rebuilding an army

even more enthusiastic than me.

"You can go on leave as from tomorrow," he said, "and you have no need to come back here as long as you get to the school on the proper day. Get your mess sergeant to pay you out and I will make out your pass, and make you corporal tomorrow."

I went back to the sergeant major, gave him the colonel's instructions, and he had to get the quartermaster sergeant to pay me out. I told him it was lucky I had not sent the second letter *[explaining to his wife that leave was cancelled]* but all he could say was, "You cunning bleeder", which I took as a compliment.

I took my leave and did the course and it was not till I rejoined the regiment that I learned that the colonel had been as good as his word, and I had been made a corporal from the day I went on leave. I passed the course with the Class One grade but the colonel was now away on a course himself, learning how to be a commanding officer. He needed that course as much as I needed mine, but I suppose he had to take it. So I never did get that third stripe after all.

My troop sergeant in the scout cars was more of the officer type than I was and, though he was quite capable, he knew little about scout cars. How could he? They were new vehicles. I had been on that course in France, but he had been given the job of taking over vehicles neither he nor anyone else in the regiment had seen before. Now I was his second man and, as a sergeant, slept apart from the lower ranks. I was in charge of the men most of the time, either on parade or in the living quarters. I was still not very popular with them but they came to realise that I was something like medicine: horrible but good for them.

It was midsummer when I noticed one man, when dressing, wore no underwear. I asked him why not and found that half of the men dressed the same way. They said it was too hot for underpants and could not understand my utter disgust. I made them all wear something and explained to them that wearing the same khaki serge for a year or more without it ever being cleaned would do them much more harm than a bit of heat. They did what I asked with bad grace and just thought I was being 'regimental'.

As time went on we became an efficient troop in the handling of the cars, but I was a bit worried about their prowess with small arms. Some time before, when I was still a trooper, there had been just one revolver firing practice. I still do not see the point of training men to do everything else except use their weapons. Surely the bullets expended would be no more costly than the petrol and vehicles used in the same kind of exercises week after week.

With revolver practice, the target was a man-size cut-out with a range of ten and 15 yards. In the case of well-

Rebuilding an army

trained men it might be 20 yards. A six inch square of paper was stuck in the middle of the target's body, not as a 'bull' *[bull's eye]* but as an aiming mark. Any hit on the target, even if it was just clipped, counted the same. In a real situation the target would probably be moving and if you were not moving yourself (or on a galloping horse or moving vehicle) you would most likely be out of breath or trembling with fear or excitement. So imagine these men standing still, aiming at a six foot tall target stuck in the ground ten yards away, and still missing it. Sad to say, most of them missed it with every shot.

But this short-barrelled weapon is very difficult to get used to, but I was used to it. I had had five years in the Tanks in peacetime and the old tanks helped to train us. I put six in the white paper with my right hand and four in it with my left, and I heard the sergeant major in charge asking, "Who is that man?" But I had had the training. It was the first and last time in England for these men.

Later, when I was troop sergeant in the desert, I called the lads together and explained that if any one of them came upon an enemy and the two of them were similarly armed, they would be very annoyed if they were the ones to get killed. I gave them *carte blanche* with their weapons. There were plenty of kite-hawks about and I told them that as long as they brought me back the empty cases I would replenish their stock. I remember one man very proudly bringing me some feathers from

Rebuilding an army

one kite-hawk he had shot with his revolver and I doubt if I could have done that myself.

Back in England, my troop sergeant made no secret of the fact that he was after a commission and at last he left us. I don't know what happened; I never saw him again. I hope he did well.

I was now left as the top man in the ranks. There was a Scottish lieutenant in charge of the troops and I had to act as sergeant. The pair of us never did hit it off very well but he was a good man in his own way. (Later, in the desert, he tried to win the war on his own. He was very conscientious and if he had lived would probably have earned a Victoria Cross, but he was killed in action a short while after I was invalided back.)

Eventually the order came for us to take the scout cars to Woolwich to be painted with desert colours so we knew we would be on our way soon. We travelled from somewhere near Devizes to Woolwich. I had worked from Plumstead bus garage before the war, when I was still buying a house at Sidcup. I told the lieutenant I knew the way but as a matter of pride he insisted on leading us till we got to the Orpington by-pass and then he had to give up. My house was just off the main road but we went past the back of it. I knew my wife was not there but I wished some of my neighbours might have looked out.

In the canteen wich I was somewhat put out when the girl behind the counter treated me in exactly the same manner as she treated all the 'base wallahs'. Could she not see that we were about to join the Eighth Army, probably going to our deaths? But she couldn't. I should think she is still in the same grade now; that type do not deserve promotion.

Shortly after that all vehicles were driven up to Manchester to embark on the ship canal. I thought this was a very cunning idea on someone's part; we were sailing from another port. But first we were going on four days leave, the final one.

We were paid out ready to leave as soon as we liked the next morning, but we had to spend the night in a dance hall in Lunar Park. I had a fearful cold and one blanket. I looked at the bare boards of the floor in our sleeping quarters, with no heat, and decided that if I just lay down, by the morning I would have pneumonia. I did not want to go out, who does with one of those colds? But I decided to go and get as much whisky inside me as I could. Fancy seeing my wife for the last time, at least till the war was over, in the condition I was in!

I had plenty of money, about £4 for the four days, and whisky was 2/6 *[12.5 pence]* a double. I spent 17/6 *[88 pence]* for doubles and decided I should eat something to keep me sober. I walked round till I found a fish bar and had a good late supper, a thing I very seldom do. Even now I rarely eat after 7 o'clock. Then I thought I had better have one for the road and had another half a

Rebuilding an army

crown's *[2s 6d/12.5p]* worth. Before I left I met one of my troop. He wanted to treat me (I must have been getting more popular). As I was on doubles I treated him then went 'home'. I slept like a log and in the morning was as right as rain. My wife met me at Middlesbrough station and told me I stank of whisky; and this was two o'clock the next afternoon.

There was one little thing that happened before this. The troop lieutenant called me aside one day and told me that the troop had approached him in a body and asked him if he could get rid of me as they could not stick me much longer. He told me that he had thought it over and decided to take no action. In the desert six months later the troop spokesman approached me and told me what they had done and then added that now they were glad that I was still with them. That was the best compliment ever paid me.

About the time we were preparing to leave for the desert I was appointed lance sergeant and had three stripes on my arm once more. This was an unpaid rank and it annoyed me that I was doing a job which at the start of the war carried the rank of warrant officer III and I was not even a sergeant.

We boarded the liner 'Orion' at Glasgow and that was goodbye to England for a bit. On board I found my old chess-playing friend, Stan. He was also wearing three stripes, and was now senior to me. We played a lot of chess on the ten week voyage round the Cape but in the meanwhile I had other duties thrust upon me.

I was made mess deck sergeant, a kind of permanent orderly sergeant. I did not think that this was quite fair as I had no more experience of boats than a lot of the regular sergeants whose job I was doing. I had thought a ship had a deck purely to keep the waves from going inside it, and it had not occurred to me that there was anything underneath it. I found out that there were decks, one below the other, right down under the sea, and in our case they were all occupied by troops. I think there were more than 4,000 souls on that boat, and that included a handful of nursing sisters.

These women, who had officer rank, were allowed to come up for air on the boat deck. They reached it by an open staircase (it may have been a companion way, but to me it was a staircase) and there was always a group of sex-hungry men waiting at the foot of the stairs, watching them go up and down. On one occasion I saw a nurse take her top coat off and, with an exaggerated gesture, hold it round her legs as she came down. This gave the troops a big laugh, though she had not meant it that way.

My job as mess deck sergeant took a lot of loose time off my hands, but the sergeants also had to do a deck patrol at night. There was strictly no smoking after the sun went down and any light was to be shot out, by order. That included cigarettes. This caused a never to be forgotten sight. As we neared the tropics the deck was crowded with silent men in the pitch dark watching for the sun to rise. As soon as the tip of the sun showed, there would be the sound of hundreds of matches being struck together. In one minute the sun seemed to shoot up from the sea, and it was another day.

We were sailing two abreast in line and the old 'Orion' was the leader of her line. We had paravenes[1] out each side to ward off any mines there may have been. If there were any we missed them. I was struck by the marvellous 'station' the other boats kept. One night as the light went I happened to be on deck patrol; I took a line with my eye to the ship level with us which was at least a mile away. At dawn, as it became visible, I took the same sight and that ship was in exactly the same position.

On another occasion I was watching the same boat. It was a lovely afternoon with nothing happening when without any warning a door opened in the side of that boat and a coffin slid out. That was all. It was too far away to know if there was a ceremony. I just saw the thing happen.

One night when I was not on patrol I was called urgently to the top deck. The sergeants on duty were grouped together and wanted my advice on a light they could see. It looked to be a lamp swinging from a mast of the ship in front of us, quite bright, and they were

[1] *A towed underwater minesweeping device.*

Rebuilding an army

undecided whether to shoot it out. I looked at it and it took a minute for the truth to sink in. We were the leading ship, therefore it could not be a lamp. We were in the tropics; it was a star. I felt as foolish as they did, but they would have looked even sillier if they had tried to shoot it. We could now read by starlight, as we could later in the desert.

I found I was a good sailor and liked a bit of rough weather. Once we had quite a storm and I went right into the bow and stood there till it was over. There did not seem to be another soul in the world but I enjoyed the experience. I was also fascinated by the fact that at night I could look so far down into the sea. It was strange to see the host of fish of all kinds lit by their own phosphorescence flitting about at different levels. We also often saw flying fish during the day.

The Navy were with us all the way. There were a lot of us and I suppose the tanks were in the same convoy. I was surprised at the small size of the fighting ships. From my liner a cruiser looked such a small thing. But as it was really a floating gun bearer, the less target it presented the better. But how efficient these boats looked – and were!

Various activities were organised on board to keep the troops amused, and one of these was a tug-of-war competition. Each sergeant had to coach his own troop and that included me. Now whether it was by accident or

Rebuilding an army

design (because of the small size of our vehicles) all my men were small. The heavies were in the motor transport, and I could see that if my troop was to be in the running we should have to use our brains. I gave the team a secret talk and instilled into them the need to obey my instructions implicitly. Some of the teams were not even 'sized' and that helped.

The 'pulls' were necessarily parallel with the run of the boat and my plan was to pull as the boat pitched. During the ten weeks we had about six contests, and in the semi-finals we were up against the motor transport heavies. We pulled downhill and we held uphill. As the boat pitched we worked with it and we beat them. We arrived in port before the final so the ultimate winners were never determined. But we were congratulated for what we had done.

Nothing exciting occurred on the voyage, though we did find things a bit strange while afloat. We had to get used to washing in salt water and had to use a special soap. The canteen was open for only one hour each morning and sold no drink of any kind. So the lads bought the next best thing: large tins of pears, of which there seemed to be an unlimited quantity. These tins were capable of holding at least a quart of water. One man reported sick with a bad stomach, then admitted to having bought six of these tins the day before and eating the lot himself.

Rebuilding an army

This was an example of why people in my position are always watching his men: to make sure they do wear clean clothes, to ensure they wash what they take off and so on. While afloat they had to do it for themselves and a few of them had to be checked.

There was no ceremony when we crossed the Equator; in fact none of us knew exactly when that was. I do remember that it was so hot that the wax in my ears melted. We berthed near Freetown *[capital of Sierra Leone]* one afternoon, and now and then I could see a man riding a camel going on his way. Nothing could be seen of the place itself but after giving it a long, hard look I decided that I could now tell my grandchildren[1], if I acquired any, that I had been there.

We continued on our way down towards the Cape and one night a pal called me up on deck. Over to the west we could see a mountainous island in the moonlight.

"That's St Helena," said my friend. We thought of the dictator[2] of the previous century. He had come unstuck; let's hope ours did too. I found an old atlas and judged we were 1,000 miles from any other land. How far out that calculation was I never found out.

It was night time when we sighted Cape Town *[a coastal city in South Africa]* and seeing the place without

---

[1] *He had eight grandchildren, and at the time of going to press, seven great grandchildren.*
[2] *Napoleon was exiled on St Helena in 1815.*

Rebuilding an army

a blackout made the war seem very far away. It was too. What expectation could Hitler have of ever dropping a single bomb there?

There was great excitement on board; we all knew we planned to stop here for a few days and I was given a new job for the length of the stop. I was detailed to stay aboard in charge of the 'ack-ack[1]'. This seemed to be piling it on a bit too much and I went to see the squadron leader about it. He told me that my duties would be "four hours on and eight off", and that as the boat was only ten minutes walk from the town centre, I would see much more of the place than the others. They were going to a camp several miles away with no transport to get them into Cape Town, and they would actually be worse off. Events proved him right; they were camped in a valley, there was a downpour of rain and a lot of their kit was washed away in a flood that came through the camp.

We all received a hero's welcome from the townspeople. On the way into town we followed a trail of fruit peel and sweet wrappings covering the road. (The only comparable event I have seen since was the trail I saw left by the Aldermaston[2] marchers of recent times.) The people took us into their homes and hotels,

---

[1] *An anti-aircraft gun.*

[2] *The Aldermaston marches were organised by the Campaign for Nuclear Disarmament (CND) in the 1950s and 1960s, taking place between the Atomic Weapons Research Establishment at Aldermaston in Berkshire, and London.*

all expenses on them. We never seemed to come into contact with anyone of Dutch descent and on inquiry it was admitted that this section of the populace stayed out of the way. So it was fairly plain to see that we were getting an exaggerated welcome to spit in the Dutch eyes, so to speak. Why worry? We got the benefit.

Cape Town was a beautiful city. I understood that Smuts[1] would not allow factories to mar the landscape. The main post office was all black marble and flood lighting; I never discovered the source of the lighting though I looked long enough.

As we walked along Adderly Street, the Oxford Street of the town, we saw that each jeweller's shop displayed a watch keeping time in a glass of water to prove its reliability.

Some white inhabitants were window shopping and the police were armed with whips. If a coloured man did not give a white person the right of way, the whip was used. No whites took any notice of this, not even the women. Everywhere there were signs saying 'Whites' or 'Natives'. This included the bars and the public toilets.

There were parts of town we were not allowed to enter.

---

[1] *Field Marshal Jan Christian Smuts was a prominent South African and British Commonwealth statesman and military leader. He served as prime minister of the Union of South Africa from 1919 until 1924 and from 1939 until 1948. At this time he advocated racial segregation and opposed the enfranchisement of black Africans, though softened his view later on.*

Rebuilding an army

I decided that however well-kept the town was, it was not a place I would like to live or let my wife go out in at night.

One family that took me under their wing for the stay made a point of taking our names and addresses so they could eventually write home on our behalf. My wife received a letter from them some months later saying that I had passed through. It was a kind thought and could not have done any harm, as by the time the letter might have been read by anyone else we would have reached our destination.

Several weeks later we disembarked at Tewfic, the Port of Suez. The dry sand of the beach, pounded to a fine dust by the many bare feet that had trodden it, rose in clouds with every step taken by us or the natives who were unloading. The local beggar kids were out in force, though what they could get from us it was hard to see. I was really shocked at the way these kids ignored the flies which crawled round their eyes. Even a cow would twitch its tail but these kids just let them crawl.

Later, I learnt that these flies would go for any moist place: the sides of the mouth, eyes, nose and anywhere else. Seaside sand is washed by salt water every day but dry sand is just a breeding ground for these filthy insects. (Since then, if doing a bit of cementing at home, with the usual 'half yard' of sand, I never leave sand about uncovered and I never allow children to play with it.)

Rebuilding an army

We arrived at base camp by the 'sweet water canal'[1]. It was a canvas camp with lots of tents dead in line (as one would expect at a base). It had a guard mounted by the regiment whose place we were taking. We stayed here while the vehicles were inspected after the sea voyage and put in fighting order.

Once more the regiment had to find a peacetime soldier *[who it was supposed knew the procedure]*, so we could take over from the other regiment in the proper ceremonial manner. So I was chosen as first guard commander as I was presumed to know the drill. It also meant a frantic digging out of all our equipment and cleaning it for my guard and me, while the rest of the regiment settled down, it being the first night. While I had to admit to myself that it would not do for the other regiment to discover that their relief did not know how to take over, I promised myself that this would be the last time this happened.

In spite of the rush, I had to find time to give the men a rehearsal for the next day. Anyhow, we got there and everything proceeded calmly enough for a start.

Then the commanding officer objected to the dust being churned up by trucks passing his orderly room. This was naturally adjacent to the road, in the front line of the camp. The sand road was like the dust at Tewfic:

[1] *A canal which was dug by thousands of Egyptian fellahin peasants to facilitate the construction of the Suez Canal.*

pounded and pounded as with a pestle and mortar. The slightest movement sent up a slowly rising cloud which took minutes to settle. The trucks were all open and the drivers wore goggles. The colonel sent word to me, as the guard commander, to slow all vehicles to ten miles an hour through the camp.

Later on I saw a truck bearing down on us at a steady 40mph, and held up my arm. The driver was a captain and obviously a veteran of the desert. I saluted him, apologised and told him the colonel's orders were because of the dust. He was smothered in dust from head to foot except for when he removed his dust-covered goggles, where the space they had covered was clean. He looked surprised and indignant and appeared to be searching the area, ignoring the slowly settling dust cloud behind his truck.

"**Dust**", he said, "**What bloody dust**?" He drove off in a cloud.

When we dismounted guard I sought out my troop lieutenant and reminded him of the many extra duties I had been given and told him that the guard had settled things. I was still an unpaid lance sergeant and I gave him till the end of the week to decide: either I should be given the rank for the job or the job should be given to someone else, and I would revert to the ranks again. He did not like it and said it could not be done at such short notice. I told him that the London Transport Buses, where

Rebuilding an army

I had worked in civil life[1], made up my pay in any case, but if I did the job I wanted the rank for it. At the end of the week my lieutenant begrudgingly told me I was now a full sergeant. Maybe this was because when he approached the colonel (the same second in command), he remembered the promise he had made me back in Blighty.

Although the lads may not have known the peacetime ceremonies, they had been well schooled in the fighting methods of the desert; that is, as well as men can be when they have never fought in a desert. We all knew how to use a sun compass, how to find our way by the stars and so on. One thing was instilled into us: if we were lost at night we should not move till it was light again, as the enemy might have moved in the darkness and we might run into them. Later on one of my duties was to patrol the entire perimeter of our 'Laager'[2] to ensure no enemy was near. It was also known to all and sundry that at every battle everyone was "put in the picture".

The regiment was ready, the tanks were driven up onto their transporters and we moved out. I was with the scout cars and followed behind. We moved out onto

---

[1] *When Wally married Bel in 1936 he was a bus conducter, then later became a bus driver.*

[2] *Historically a South African encampment formed by a circle of wagons, defended against opponents.*

Rebuilding an army

the desert road, with a single track each way, leading from Alexandria to the other end of the continent, maybe 3,000 miles. We knew Jerry was 80 miles along it at El Alamein, and we did not know how near them we would be when we halted.

It was July but here that made no difference to the sun. It sets at seven o'clock in this latitude, and it was getting towards that time. One of my cars packed up and, as the sergeant, it was my duty to stay with it and get it going if possible, rejoining the column as soon as possible. As we suspected, the cause was lack of petrol and sand trouble. By the time we got the thing started once more it was dark. I was worried about filling up with petrol but I decided to obey our teaching and stay where we were till morning.

We were up early, had breakfast and were away by first light. No-one had told us a thing and I was worried about the need to fill up with petrol more than anything else. I just hoped I could find the regiment before we ran dry.

We drove a few miles up the road and I saw a scout car approaching. My first question to the driver was where could we get petrol. His answer really shook us all.

"You don't need any now, Wal," he said. "The regiment has about two tanks left." We could not believe it. We had heard nothing and had no idea that the unit was going into action. Our last sight of it was with the tanks still on the transporters. But it was true enough. Out of

Rebuilding an army

a complement of about 51 plus tanks, the regiment had only two or three left.

It was all a matter of the difference between true north and magnetic north. A horseshoe of low hills was occupied by the enemy with the dreaded '88'[1] guns and a minefield was on the flat ground. The plan had been for the tanks to advance on a track cleared of mines and marked by white tapes, but there was a mix-up over true and magnetic north, resulting in the tanks going into the minefield. As the tracks were blown off and the tanks became immobile, the 88s took them at their leisure and that was that. For months the regiment was known as the 'Minesweepers'.

However, at that time there was something else which concerned me and my troop. I acquired some petrol for both my cars and went to find my troop lieutenant. As I said earlier he was the VC type and he actually found me. He was crying, but ordered me to get all the troop of ten cars together. I asked him what he intended to do and he said he was going to take us in regardless.

"The cars are too light to be blown by the mines," he said, "the Bren gunners can keep shooting, that will keep the 88s from firing and we will get right through them." The cars weighed two and a half tons each and, having

---

[1] *The '88' was a Pak 43, a German 88mm anti-tank gun and the most powerful anti-tank gun of the Wehrmacht to see service in significant numbers during WW2.*

The Reservist 135

Rebuilding an army

had that course in England, I knew enough about the Jerry 'Teller' mine to know that the first part of his plan would not work. I wondered if he realised that the Jerry Spandeau machine gun which was superior to ours, would also be stationed with the 88s. And apart from all that, what was the purpose? If, by any blind luck, we managed to break through, we could only end up surrounded by the German army, and the scout cars would all be gone as well. Jerry would probably think it was the Charge of the Light Brigade[1] once more and, being sportsmen, would give us a burial with full honours. We would be going to our deaths and for no purpose. I did not know how to get out of it but I put on my most regimental manner and told him that I would not move the cars until he had seen the colonel.

It always happens in the army that no matter how private a conversation may be, someone knows about it. I thought that our talk had been private but somehow the lads knew. Off went the lieutenant to see the colonel and the thing was not mentioned again. Perhaps his driver had listened in when he approached the colonel but word came back that he just answered him with two words, the second one being "off".

I forgot to mention that the purpose of this adventure

---

[1] *A charge of British light cavalry led by Lord Cardigan against Russian forces during the Battle of Balaclava on 25 October 1854 in the Crimean War.*

Rebuilding an army

would have been for the honour of the regiment. Apart from the needless waste of life and equipment, in the cynical eyes of the British Army it would have made the regiment a laughing stock.

This battle became known to the regiment as the 'July Do' and we had to wait for a new lot of tanks. The day after the battle some of our missing men drifted back. They said Rommel had sent them on their way with a packet of fags, a bar of chocolate and a full bottle of water. He had told them to keep the sea on their left and let them go.

There were men wounded in the battle who were not discharged from hospital until after the next action at Alamein. Any man who was in the action zone within certain periods was allowed to wear the prized '8' on his medal ribbon. This was looked upon as the distinguishing mark between a front line man and a 'base wallah'. It seemed rather unfair that the men wounded in action at a time outside a period should be excluded, but there it was.

While the regiment was reorganising I was sent back to Cairo for a further course on mines and booby traps held on a flat piece of desert just outside Cairo within sight of the Suez road. Here we played about happily with gun cotton and detonating cord.

It amused us to watch the women workers come into town on a special bus. The road was about half a mile distant but we could see plainly enough. The bus used to stop at evidently its 'last stop before town'. The driver would get out to stretch his legs and the women, all dressed in enveloping garments, would get out and relieve themselves beside the road.

While in the Cairo barracks I met a sergeant major I had heard about years before; tales go round and round in the army. In peacetime there were four battalions of tanks which never met except perhaps on the sports field. But men went to India from each unit and stories from the units would then go round India, back to the armoured cars in Egypt, and then to the other units at home. The story about the sergeant major happened in my peacetime unit before I reached it, but I already knew about it when I arrived.

He was on a peacetime exercise and the tanks had been out for a couple of days. When the order to 'switch off' was given no-one ever knew whether it would be for five minutes or five hours. This sergeant wanted to answer the call of nature and when the order to 'switch off' came, he was out of his tank and into the woods. We all used to wear one-piece overalls with the usual equipment on top. He no sooner got settled than the order came to start up again, and he was caught with his trousers down. Dressing as quickly as he could, he hurried back to his tank. In those days, apart from the driver, the crew shared the same compartment, and it

Rebuilding an army

was not long before the sergeant could smell something. He accused the other men in turn, and it was not until later that one of them called the sergeant's attention to a piece of paper on the back of his neck. Taking into account the one-piece overalls, the rest can be guessed.

When I met him in Cairo I did not know who he was until a man (who I also did not know) said to me, "You remember the tale of so and so?" and said that this was the man concerned. I had joined that peacetime unit in 1931. It was now 1942 and he had not yet lived it down.

There was one thing on this course that was typical 'army'. On my course in England, it had been instilled into the class that no explosive should be touched with metal tools. If half a pound of gun-cotton was needed, the one pound slab had to be cut with a wooden saw so that there would be no sparks. At this camp, in a huge shed, men were dismantling mines that had been laid and picked up again. The TNT[1] had hardened and on long benches, men (smoking of course) were chipping the explosive from the cases with hammers and cold chisels.

※ ※ ※

---

[1] *Trinitrotoluene is a solid yellow chemical compound known as an explosive material with convenient handling properties. The explosive yield is considered to be the standard measure of bombs and the power of explosives.*

Desert rats

BACK TO work again: that summer in the desert I became very busy. It seems silly but, although I was the scout car man, I was also the squadron driving instructor for the tanks. My own men knew their jobs well enough and this was the time when I let them go shooting with their weapons for practice; just as well as, apart from making them more efficient, it gave them something to think about.

As I had just finished the course on mines and booby traps, the colonel thought it would be a good idea to let the rest of the regiment learn something about them too. So I took classes each afternoon, explaining how a pattern of mines could be laid, how they worked and the different kinds of booby traps the enemy might leave around. As I gave these lectures to the whole regiment, the officers first, then the rest, it took a lot of time, and the situation began to get on my nerves. I seemed to be always on the go: tanks, mines, looking after my own troop. The trouble was that I knew one particular sergeant who never did a thing. He did not happen to have a troop, he said he knew nothing and seemed to spend his time sunbathing. When I had been lecturing for two hours in the desert sun, standing shouting so that a group of 50 men could hear, the sight of this man supine made me feel so enraged that I could hardly contain myself. The job of looking after the troop was quite a thing on its own. I had to make sure they were personally clean, which they were, but I had to know. I had to see they used the sand as latrines far enough away from our vehicles, which were our living quarters. All waste food and tins had to be properly buried because of the flies, the vehicles had to be kept in fighting trim; radio, engine, guns all OK. Water was rationed to half a gallon per man per day, and had to be enough for cooking, washing, laundry, and most important, the car radiator; that came first. And I had to keep up their morale. I was over 30 and the men were about 20.

I 'invented' the desert broom: a stick with a cross-piece of wood to push the sand away from the cars and leave it nice and smooth. We did not live in our cars, there was not room, so we slept, washed and ate all around them. Imagine the dirt in the form of crumbs of food, cigarette ends, washing and spitting that could accumulate in a day. Then think of the flies. If we had a mug of tea, no matter how hot the tea or the tin mug, the rim of the mug would be one mass of flies. The tea was drunk while continually waving the free hand across the top of the mug, and even then the more knowing flies just leaned backwards and hung on. In conditions like that it was as well to have a new floor every day. When I first introduced that broom it was jeered at as 'bull', but it soon became very popular.

Desert rats

We stayed at this spot in the "blue" for several weeks. We were issued with picnic stoves operated by petrol under pressure and as at this time we didn't have bread, we tried to cook the hard tack biscuits in several different ways. I tried to stew them with corned beef, or to curry them, but they always seemed to finish up tasting the same. The petrol came in expendable four-gallon tins, and these gave me a good idea; I made an oven with one of them. My wife had shown me how to make rice pudding and these became locally famous. Even other troops sent over a mess tin full of rice and their own tin of milk.

The petrol tins had another use. We took two tins, cut the top and bottom out of them and sunk one in the ground so the top was just level with the surface. Then we placed the second on top of the first and there was a beautiful toilet. It was better than getting a spade, rushing away from everything, digging a hole, using it and covering it up again. But the tin was sharp so I procured some packing case wood, a hacksaw blade, pencil and piece of string. After an hour's work and a couple of blisters I had a perfect seat. As no-one else seemed to be handy with a hacksaw blade I made a couple more. When we moved, the seats were taken with us and one man actually reported to me that his seat had been rendered useless by enemy action.

While we were camped at this place we were still aware

Desert rats

of the war. Jerry sent his planes to shoot us up at sunset and my troop received its first casualty from one of these. It dropped a light bomb, blowing a man under his car. The cars only had a ground clearance of ten inches.

This incident brought home the fact that it was not all one big joke, any more than the late disaster when all those tanks were lost. At the next sunset the men were all ready and took cover in time.

I am no more a hero than the next man and took up a position behind a car and fired over the top, but my gun jammed and the planes were gone. I had expected the others to be doing the same and when I saw the passive role they had taken, I thought back to the road to Dunkirk when I had hidden under a tank for a similar reason.

I called them together and explained that we were the only people in the regiment to be issued with the 100 round magazines for the Bren guns and we were expected to use them. I also told them that if they "had a go" they would feel better and if Jerry found his reception too hot he would go to an easier target. The next attack found them defending and after that they started looking forward to it. In a matter of three days It was strange to see the looks of expectancy with which they waited and the disappointment if the planes did not come.

It was my duty to drive full circle round the regiment to ensure that Jerry had not moved up in the night. One morning just before sunrise I was doing the round as

Desert rats

usual when my driver and I were bombed, just us. There was no-one else moving and the pilot must have seen our exhaust pipe or the glowing smoke from it. They were only small bombs and the first dropped 50 yards in front. It was simple to dodge them as the plane had to circle each time and at the exact second we swung right or left and he missed. I am partly colour blind but those bombs burning the sand and sending it up in showers was a wonderful sight. As far as I could tell there were all shades of purple and blues mingling. He soon gave up and I thought that it must be a privilege to be the only one to be a target.

Another time, at sunset, I had to go to the ration truck for regular supplies. The truck happened to be due east from my troop and, with my arms full of rations, I saw the planes come out of the west, dropping their bombs in a straight line right towards my men. In between the troop and where I stood some 200 yards away was one of the tin box conveniences, with a man using it. I saw him stand up as a bomb fell. When I reached him with my arms full of food he was OK, but though the tins were still in position there was a hole 20 feet long sideways from it. As the bomb fell the pilot must have turned right to avoid him. In the bomb pit was a quantity of what looked like broken glass; that was created by the heat of the bomb burning the sand.

The regiment had been re-equipped and now had the

Desert rats

full complement of tanks once more, but they were all old ones. Mostly they were the Valentines which we had had previously but there were also some General Grants which I should think the Yanks were glad to get rid of. These had two main guns, one on each side of the main structure of the tank. To use them the tank had to be swung round to face the target, which was slow and awkward. We had a few of another type of tank which had a radial engine; cylinders in a circle. It was stressed to us that before starting one of these engines, the thing had to be turned by hand at least twice full circle to ensure that oil seeping into the lower cylinders would not cause a hydrostatic lock. If you were in a hurry, then good luck.

But mainly this was a quiet time and we were getting four days leave in turn to Cairo. It was a time of little things and little observations. One day there was rain for perhaps 30 minutes. Not heavy, just a light shower, the only one we had. When it stopped the desert was covered with little blue flowers. In an hour or two they had faded and gone. And the desert rats, the Jerboah or kangaroo rats that people believe almost crowded us out, were actually very few. I do not think I saw more than two and they were just fleeting glimpses. One was sitting on its haunches then suddenly disappeared. It had taken one great jump and remained still on landing. Its colour was a perfect blend with the sand, I had no idea which

Desert rats

way it had jumped and I never saw it again.

A rather unusual procedure was when the regimental padre did his rounds he collected empty beer bottles. The bottles were used when he buried the dead, which was one of his duties. When he found a corpse he would take any papers there were on it, bury the man if possible (temporarily), make a roll of the papers and push them inside a beer bottle. The bottle would then be pushed into the ground as a grave marker, and when the Graves Commission eventually came along they were able to find the body as well as the identification, intact in the bottle.

The bottles were from the mobile canteens that used to come several times a week. They came up in a 'light skinned' vehicle into the forward areas and faithfully brought us cigarettes, razor blades etc. I am a pipe smoker and though I smoke an ounce a day, I always had enough tobacco. Finding pipes was more of a problem but I was able to scrounge them from men who had tried smoking one but had given up.

The squadron leader also smoked a pipe and he told me that on his leave in Cairo he had seen a favourite English pipe in a shop window. Forgetting for a minute that Cairo was not England he rushed in and told them to wrap it up. They made such a to-do of wrapping it that too late he wondered about the price. When finally they handed it to him in a fancy-wrapped box tied with special ribbon, he said he did not like to quibble when

Desert rats

he was charged 1,000 rupees, or £10. He never used that pipe as he was frightened of breaking it. We were also given a free issue of 'V' cigarettes which were so horrible that they were smoked only as a last resort. One day I overheard two men. It transpired that neither had smoked for two days. One asked the other if he had any cigarettes. The other said no but he had some 'V's in his pack that the other was welcome to. The first man refused them.

It was about this time I got my four days leave in Cairo. I went with a man I am still friendly with 30 years later. His name was Frank and, though he had a perforated ear drum and need not have been a front line man, he took over as troop sergeant when I left. My pal Stan also came along and this made a great difference. Going to a strange town in a foreign land, mooching round on one's own is not much fun.

After finding a hotel we explored together. During the four days we saw the main sights and included a trip to the theatre where there was an English singer. She wore an evening gown with no shoulder straps, the first one we had seen. Reaching up to it with both hands and pulling, she said, "All right boys, it won't come down".

We saw 'Mrs Miniver'[1] in a cinema with a slide back

---

[1] *A 1942 American romantic war drama directed by William Wyler and starring Greer Garson and Walter Pidgeon, inspired by the 1940 novel 'Mrs Miniver' by Jan Struther.*

Desert rats

Wally (left), Frank and a scout car in 1943.

roof, and had our fortunes told in the Blue Mosque. I had mine told twice, once by stones thrown on the ground and once by scribe marks in the sand. The first cost five rupees and I was given a life of 35 years; the second was seven rupees and I was given 37[1] years. They are both right to date. One did tell me I would not be wounded but would be sent home with some hurt to my head. He was right: I was sent home by the psychiatrists.

On the first day I went to a big store that specialised in sending gifts home for us. They said they would get your gift through the customs and if you returned the next day they would show you the receipt to prove the gift was on its way home. I bought a leather handbag and a silk handkerchief and was duly shown the documents that proved the goods were dispatched. When I arrived

[1]*Wally lived to be 89 so he had about another 59 years - Ed.*

Desert rats

Wally (left) with Stanley and Jack in Cairo on Christmas Day 1942.

home two years later, my wife showed me the bag with the handkerchief inside. The bag she received was three inches long and would have cost about two rupees. The bag I had paid for cost about 400 rupees. It was a clever little scheme and typical of the people.

In Cairo I soon realised that the Cairenes did not consider the war was anything to do with them. There also seemed to be two classes: the rich and the poor. The rich women with their dyed blonde Marcell-waved[1] hair spoke French and the poor spoke Arabic. It reminded me of what England must have been like at the time of the Norman Conquest, when the rich used French and the serfs spoke Anglo Saxon.

In the cinema the use of three languages gave a curious

[1] *Tight waves given to the hair by means of heated curling irons, popular from the 1920s to the 1950s.*

result. On the screen there would be an English picture *[film]* and naturally the characters would be speaking English or American. At the bottom of the screen there was the French translation and running vertically down the side was the Arabic one. The dialogue on screen would perhaps make the English laugh, then seconds later the French would have the same laugh, though the action had now changed. Then later still the Arabs would get it and they would laugh in their turn. This could make us laugh again as the theme of the story could now be quite different.

The Cairo trams interested me a lot. They were single deckers with three trailers with open sides and running boards the length of the coach, and two boards as steps so one could get on from the road at a place where a seat was available. The conductor had a little curved horn and would lean out of whatever coach he was in and blow it to signal for the driver to move. The coaches were only coupled together and the conductor had to swing round on the outside from one coach to the next to collect the fares.

There seemed to be a rule that any person riding on the running board went free, and the running boards often held more passengers than the tram. The up and down tracks were just as close together as in Britain and I was really frightened the first time I saw two trams approaching each other. They were going quite fast and

Desert rats

the two running boards of each tram were crowded with people. With their flowing robes blowing in the breeze they seemed to take up more room than they actually did. Watching them hurtling together, it looked to me as if all these people would be rubbed off by each other as they passed. But they weren't. It was like two sheets of corrugated iron passing each other; everyone held on, they all rubbed shoulders and it seemed to be nothing unusual. The drawback was that the trams encouraged thieves. They scrutinised the passengers, leaped on the tram at the right place, snatched whatever possessions they had spotted and were off again. Lots of men lost their hats like this and Stan lost his '21st' gold watch, pulled off his wrist. He did get off to follow the thief but it was hopeless in the little streets.

We were constantly annoyed by the boot boys. These kids, in pairs or more, threw their soft 'blacking' at your boots, more often than not splashing your clothes as well. Then the second one would chase the first away and offer to clean your boots. You were blackmailed into paying, as otherwise you would have to walk with a kind of black snowball on your boot.

I did not have a big opinion of these people nor their country. One of the early civilisations, they now had no language and no writing[1]. The basic coin was a piastre

[1]*Wally perhaps not seeing beyond his own interactions in Cairo here. - Ed*

The Reservist 151

Desert rats

From left: Stan, Big Jack, Frank and Wally in Cairo in May 1943. Wally stayed friends with Stan and Frank for the rest of his life.

and yet there was not such a coin minted. A two-piastre piece, yes. Half of that was ten millemes.

Although there was a servility about the vendors and the café waiters, they could not be trusted. If you ordered a pot of tea in a café but did not keep a close watch, the waiter would whip the pot away and sell it to the next customer. The excuse was that he thought you were finished.

I did notice the absence of service women in town; with Jerry so near they had been moved out. Another interesting fact was that Cairo was where most deserters were caught. They called themselves the "free British" and now and then all leave would be stopped and the

Desert rats

free British would be collected.

Back with the lads again, there was talk of how someone could take a truck and drive right out of the war zone. My troop and I were discussing this on the day before August Bank Holiday. I said anyone could do it; who was to stop them? They could just take a vehicle, drive down the road and that would be that.

Every morning the radio had to be tested, and the next morning my driver said that the set was not working properly and he had better take the car to the signals for a check over. I took out my own gear from the car and he drove away. The scout car was recovered from Cairo a few days later but the driver was not found for quite a few weeks.

I met him again after Alamein at his court martial, where I was a witness. I think we were in Tunis. We were sitting outside the court martial tent and I asked him how he had lived. He said he had sold the watch I had lent him (an issue one) and had gone to various army places and scrounged tea and cakes from other soldiers. He had also gone to Suez and lived in a camp there and even lined up and drawn pay.

He was given about two years, but six months later rejoined us in Italy. He came to see me the first day and while we were talking there was a distant rumble of gunfire. When I told him what the noise was he said, "I'm not stopping here." I never saw him again.

Desert rats

We could still enjoy some leisure time and were approached one day by a guide who suggested showing us round the pyramids. The man said he would conduct a tour for 20 men for 50 piastres each. Twenty men were soon forthcoming and the trip was arranged for the following Sunday. The guide met us at an agreed tram stop. He was of a commanding appearance in his Arab gear and carefully collected the 50 piastres from each of us before we boarded a tram. In our ignorance we thought that we had paid for everything, but we soon learned that this was not the case. The tram conductor approached us for the fares and we waved him over to the guide. With a broad smile the guide waved him back. "You pay," he said cheerfully. So we paid, as the conductor insisted and after all we were riding on his tram.

The guide was quite a likeable bloke, He told me he had lived in Manchester some years ago and worked on boats on the Manchester Ship Canal. On arrival at the tram terminus he said that now we were all to travel by camel. Cheop's Pyramid[1] looked to be only a few hundred yards away but, like sheep, we went over to the camels. We all paid again but began to see the joke. I believe he got a rake-off from the camel owners.

[1] *Also known as the Great Pyramid of Giza or of Khufu, Cheops is the oldest and largest of the three pyramids in the Giza pyramid complex.*

Desert rats

The trip to the Pyramids in 1942. Wally is on the second camel from right in front. The guide told them he had been working on the Manchester Ship Canal before the war.

I had not realised how steeply a camel's back inclines when one gets up or down. If it did not have a hump one would fall off. I started off with the camel's owner walking beside me. He asked me if I would like the thing to run and I said I would. He then told me the word to make it stop as it would outrun him. Then, giving the word of command, he set the camel running. I forgot the word and would probably have ended up at Alamein on it if the owner, with visions of his property falling into enemy hands, had not exerted himself enough to catch up. The guide did not leave the tram stop. Why should he? There were plenty of 'priests' who conducted the tours, and he had 1,000 piastres to spend. Though he did have the decency to wait and conduct us back to town.

We found that the Pyramid of Cheops, which looks so smooth in pictures, was in fact stepped with huge blocks of stone. Throughout their existence they have been continually climbed. The locals made a living by putting

Desert rats

on races to the top for the benefit of tourists, from whom they took a whip-round for the winner. Obviously there could be no profit for the losers and that would mean no races, so they must have arranged for a new winner every day or shared the take.

After Alamein my regiment came back to within five miles of the pyramids. We could see them quite plainly to the east. If you looked towards them at sunset the light and shade showed trails like rabbit runs to the summit.

The Sphinx also had something that does not show up in pictures, and that was a broken nose. I was told that Napoleon caused a cannon to be fired at it so even he was small-minded about some things.

We were met at the pyramid by one of the 'priests' who conduct the tours. They were called priests as they were dressed like our own clergy, in long black coats with a white shirt collar showing. Owing to the war there was no electric light inside and our priest had a flare of magnesium. He explained that this flare was very expensive and we were to have a quick look round as he could not afford to burn it for very long. We groped our way inside and he said, "You are now in the King's Chamber. I am about to light the flare, have a quick look round NOW." He then lit the flare and said, "I am now putting the flare out," and we were in semi-darkness again.

In the flash of light we had been allowed, I had seen

the square, sombre chamber and the beautifully tooled blocks of stone that formed the roof and walls, and the air vent that someone had thought of all those thousands of years before. We then went up a stairway to the smaller Queen's Chamber, where we were once more privileged enough to be allowed the flare.

Stumbling up the stairs we had struck matches, and I was reminded of the London tube escalators. There was a flat slide of stone at balustrade height, parallel with the stairs. At intervals there were small holes in it. We were told that the coffin was pushed up the slope and a peg inserted in a hole to hold it while its pusher rested. This seemed to me a lot of trouble and design for just one corpse.

We did not ride the camels back to the tram and the priest followed us all the way to the terminus demanding money. We passed him to our guide and it was a case of thief catch thief. He got nothing from him either.

The Arabs ignored the war. One day we saw a party of them travelling west. In spite of such hazards as minefields, they just went straight through our lines and then Jerry's. The ground was not like the sand on a beach. It was hard with little stones scattered about. There were two men and two women. The men rode donkeys, like chaises longues, sitting on the rump with their legs more or less stretched along the donkeys' backs. They carried open sun shades and each led a

Wally (bottom left) and crew after Alamein.

second animal to change over to when the first one got tired. Twenty yards to the rear came the women, walking barefoot over the hard and hot terrain and each carrying an enormous bundle wrapped up in a black sheet.

On another day a party of Arabs mounted on camels attempted to cross our lines. To our surprise and amusement a second lieutenant tried to stop them. There was an argument which lasted ten minutes then they were allowed to go on. It turned out that they had previously buried fodder for the camels somewhere in front of us and needed to recover it. They reached the middle of 'No man's land' and started to dig, with no maps or anything to refer to, and brought up the fodder. The camels were fed and then they went on.

When I say there was nothing to refer to, I mean no prominent objects to identify. Our maps had a 'lone tree' marked on them. I eventually came to this 'tree'. It was a

Desert rats

bush on its own about three feet high. The only thing we could go on was the shape of the ground and the maps had the contours marked every ten feet.

One day the senior colonel sent for me and my car to take him on a drive. We did not go far and when we got out the colonel said, "I want you to take notice of the terrain; Rommel is coming this way." He took a few observations and marked his map, and we went back. A few days later Rommel attacked.

His attack was due east and he was south of us, sweeping for Egypt. Our army pressed south, squeezing him between us and the Quattarra Depression[1]. My regiment faced south and the first we saw of the enemy was two of our own Crusader tanks leading his column. If Rommel hoped to surprise us by this ruse he was wrong. As he was expected these tanks were soon out of action. I admired the tank crew of the first of these. With no hope they dismounted with their kit, piled it in front of them and made a last stand. Their tank was used for target practice and the crew died behind their pathetic barricade.

That night we stayed where we were, deployed for further action, but the enemy had retired. However, enemy planes flew over us all night and, knowing our position, the rear gunners fired as they went over. I was

---

[1] *A vast uninhabited desert that lies on average 60m below sea level.*

lying on one side of the scout car and my driver on the other. I had a blanket over my face because of the flies. My driver suddenly said that he was getting in the car but all I could think of was that it was a sight more comfortable at the side where you could stretch your legs out. But I found I could not sleep. The machine guns from the planes kept on and on. They seemed to be flying round in continuous circles. I took the blanket from my face and had the surprise of my life. I had thought it was pitch dark on the ground and that we were therefore hidden from the air, but it was as light as day. There were parachute flares hanging all over the sky and the planes were the ones in the dark, above them. I got in the car with my driver.

In the morning the battle was over. The tanks were in triangular formation, and I needed to respond to a call of nature. Another man felt the same and from our respective vehicles we took spades and, moving away, we squatted down, both facing the same way. They say Jerry has no sense of humour but one lone flyer, seeing those two backsides shining in the sun, swooped low between us. He nearly hit the sand but did not fire a shot. He was substituting for toilet paper and must have flown away laughing his head off.

Later that day I was sent forward on watch with another car. I had to pass close to the enemy Crusader tank I mentioned and as we drove past we saw the dead

Desert rats

crew at close quarters. The corpses were black with flies and with exposure to the sun, and that one had only one leg. I stayed on watch half a mile further on till the infantry came up two days later. Using my glasses I watched them come and saw them look at the tank crew's remains with interest. One man went through their pockets and, to my disgust, he then searched for the missing leg and searched the pocket still attached to it.

That was Rommel's last fling. He did reach Egypt but only the desert part. For miles back the ground was littered with his vehicles.

Some days later there was an unusual incident. The unit had been on the move and the scout cars were in a diamond formation on the back slope of a hill, with the tanks a bit further back. My scout car lieutenant took me on foot up the hill and at the top my lieutenant and I could see across a small valley, On the opposite slope were about 100 men furiously digging trenches. I could hardly believe it.

"They are Jerries, aren't they?" I asked, and the lieutenant nodded. As we watched them at work, I realised we had been joined by most of the officers from the tanks. They were standing in a group, about 30 of them, talking, laughing and pointing as if it were a great joke. I turned to my lieutenant and pointed out that Jerry was actually within hearing distance.

"Come on," I told him, "they *[the officers]* have made us

an obvious target." We had not gone ten yards from the top when there came the chatter of machine guns, and those idiots scattered like rabbits. Then Jerry realised there must be armour over the ridge and started shelling. My scout cars were in the thick of it and the colonel shouted up to me, "Get them back, Harmer."

Most of them needed only a wave of my arm but it was different with my friend Frank, who was deaf in one ear. He was at the side of his car with his headphones to his good ear, trying to tune in his radio. He was oblivious to the noise around him and took no notice of my shouting. It was only when I reached him, shook his shoulder and called him by name that he looked up. He was still concentrating on the radio and turned to me, saying he could not get it quite right. I said, "Get out of it, Frank" and he did, followed closely by me. On my run over to him I had been blown over by a near-miss shell. They were only armour-piercing ones so did not throw shrapnel or explosives around, but the force of the impact blew me down and I fell flat on my nose which was scratched on a stone on impact. That was my only war wound.

Later I saw the artillery shell the Jerry position, and the hill slope with the trenches seemed to boil. It looked like a huge bowl of porridge bubbling; every bit of it seemed to be on the move. When that was over Jerry was still there practically intact. The angle of the trenches was so different from the angle of the falling shells that though

Desert rats

it must have been uncomfortable, the shelling did no real damage. They were gone next day; they must have moved out in the night.

About this time there was quite a lot of air activity, and it seemed that our fighters had the better of it. For several days we witnessed dog fights overhead and parachute descents by the losers.

One day we could see a parachutist coming down about a mile in front of us. Suddenly our colonel's jeep started up and raced forward. In the distance another unit's jeep was doing the same thing. If the descending Jerry was looking, he may have wondered which one would get him, and why the vicious race to take one prisoner. Our unit won. He hardly had time to divest himself of his nice nylon 'chute before it was grabbed, bundled and stowed in the jeep, and the jeep was on its way back. The man was left for the other jeep to pick up. Nylon was much prized by the ladies back home suffering from clothes rationing.

With Rommel retired to lick his wounds, things eased up again and the most important events were the little normal ones of living: receiving our mail and drawing rations. The method of ration issuing was a joke. As I have pointed out, everything was done on a day to day basis but, at the same time, each vehicle had to have a further ration for the number of men with that vehicle. If a tank or car was separated from the main body by

Desert rats

breakdown, such as when I stopped before the 'July do' or when I was on that watch after Rommel's push, then you needed the food with you. The quartermaster would dish me out rations for 20 men and I had to split it into twos. I was once given a tin of jam which I estimated weighed 28lbs. I was told that if anyone wanted jam they were to come to me. As soon as the tin was opened it would be full of flies and all we could do was to give out as much as possible straight away then bury the rest. The sugar would be doled out to me by the army mugful and in turn I would measure it out in spoonfuls with the troop watching closely, counting and noting if the spoon was heaped or flat: when there is nothing else happening things like this become of major importance. But none of this careful allotting was ever carried out with a set of scales. None were issued. The quartermaster had an official list of every food item and the weight each man was entitled per day. I asked him if his list included salt and pepper; someone had even worked that out. I forget which was which but one was one 250th and the other 400th of an ounce.

One Saturday morning my lieutenant informed me that he and I were going to inspect some minefields in front of the Australian division on our right. This meant we would be away till Sunday night, though we only had to travel a few miles. We had to detour with the scout car which I was driving back to El Alamein station and then forward along the road parallel with the rail to the next station, Tel el Lisa. I do not know why the battle to come was named after Alamein when our line was in front of the next station up. There were no buildings at either place except the wooden shacks of the stations themselves, and the desert around them looked exactly the same.

At the side of the road between the two stations was a notice board. It was erected on two posts and was painted black. Stencilled on it in white paint was the question, "Do you know where you are?". There was another one after half a mile, halfway up a hill and where we were turning off the road for the station. It had a neat row of dresser hooks screwed to it and on each hook was a little white painted cross hanging by a screw-eye. Underneath the crosses was stencilled, 'If you are going past here, take one of these with you'. After the battle I saw the board with its crosses lying on the ground.

We found the Aussies' HQ under a huge camouflage of canvas and netting supported by large chunks of railway line. There were even trucks underneath it. It was pointed out to us that Jerry could observe all from the rising ground forward.

We were told to put the car under the canvas or else it would attract attention, and after that we had to wait for the morning. Then we met two officers, and one, a young captain, cheerfully told us that he did not know the layout of the minefield but if we followed his steps we

Desert rats

should be OK. Officers go first into danger so I followed and wondered whether to keep close up or stay at a distance. I was in the same quandary as a driver behind a learner at traffic lights on a hill. Do you keep very close so that if the learner lets it run back there is not much damage? Or do you keep well away so you don't get hit at all? I chanced it and kept close behind, though both the officers were lean, fit men and would not have been much of a shield.

We went right through to 'no man's land' and I could see an enemy soldier half a mile away in a long grey coat evidently inspecting his mines. We all ignored each other; after all it was Sunday morning. While out there the Aussie captain pointed out two things: a hill, one of several behind the enemy front line, and a railway cutting. The hill used to have one of the big oil drums at its summit and this had become so well known as a reference point that it was marked on the local maps. Jerry had realised this and one morning it had disappeared. This put all the maps out as no-one now knew which was 'Drum Knoll'.

The cutting was a grimmer story. As it led straight towards the enemy I could not see why it had been used, but the captain said that his infantry had used it to try to surprise the enemy. Jerry could see straight down it and it was filled with the corpses of the attackers. For some reason both sides had the 'needle' *[being obstinate]* and

Desert rats

the Germans would not allow a burial party to come near. Why this was I do not know as there is generally no malice between opposing sides. Usually each considers that the other is in the same boat and a prisoner would generally be offered a smoke. The same treatment would be given to a shot-down pilot in spite of the damage he might have just caused.

The sequel to this cutting episode is that in 1974 I read in a daily paper that a man in Australia had just been cleared of a cowardice charge which referred to his not returning to this same cutting at the time.

We returned to our unit not much the wiser as far as the mines were concerned. Everyone knew the minefield was there and we were still ignorant of the way it was laid out. This was the period when my lieutenant decided to do things off his own bat *[without consultation]*, and he used to take his driver out in front of the mines, driving up and down in 'no man's land' making his own observations. If Jerry machine-gunned the car, he would tell the driver, "Go quicker, they won't hit us." To my mind he was risking himself, the driver and the car for no purpose. This was proved a little later when General Montgomery[1]

[1] *Field Marshal Bernard Law Montgomery, nicknamed "Monty", was a senior British Army officer who fought in both the First and Second World Wars. During the Second World War he commanded the British Eighth Army from August 1942 in the Western Desert until the final Allied victory in Tunisia in May 1943. This command included the Second Battle of El Alamein, a turning point in the Western Desert Campaign.*

The Reservist

Desert rats

issued maps of the front line which pin-pointed every German machine gun nest, let alone the bigger weapons.

While mentioning the General, I will admit that I did not like him. But when I think back to Vimy and the wicked carnage there *[see p38]*, I will say that if it had not been for his insistence on a strength that would make sure of victory before he attacked, I probably would not have lived through Alamein.

It was now becoming obvious that this battle was imminent. This is when the various tracks were put down *[see p74]*. The sand was mixed into a temporary cement which was used to make the tracks. These were parallel with the road, about 100 yards apart, going up to the enemy lines. The posts with the signs on them, a cut out of a ship, hat, sun, moon, star, and so on, had to be learned by me in my scout car job. I had to know which track was for tanks, which for supplies, which to take back the wounded, which for crippled vehicles, and to be able to direct traffic to each as required.

In the background there rose two pylon-like structures with a platform on top which was protected with sandbags. These were observation posts and I thought the observers would have a rough time. But I was wrong; these things had been erected some distance back, positioned to just look over the skyline. After the battle, when I looked back at them from what had been the Jerry position, they appeared as two boxes on the skyline

Desert rats

and if shells had been fired at them they would have fallen far short. They would not be much troubled by aircraft either, as the following will demonstrate.

The whole regiment was assembled (which up till now would not have been done during daylight) for a 'putting in the picture' lecture by the brigadier. The army world is a small one and the brigadier had been my captain and adjutant in 1929 when he had signed my discharge papers from the Middlesex. Some aircraft flew over and we all looked up. "You have no need to worry", he smiled, "they are all ours now." We did not quite believe him and later when the enemy threw us a few bombs to share out we would say, "They are all ours now, the brigadier said so."

The brigadier then told us that Jerry had ten days supply of ammunition and when that was used up they would have to go back.

"Gone are the days of the cardboard tank *[life-size decoy tank made of cardboard]*, he knows all those dodges now," he told us, "We have to give him real tanks as targets and you have the oldest tanks. So you will stand on the ridge for ten days and make him expend his supplies, and then the new tanks will go through and push him out of the country." And that's what my poor old regiment did. It offered itself as a target for the duration of the battle. There were three fighting squadrons commanded by three majors. They were all killed during that time and the senior colonel was so badly wounded that when he visited the regiment a year later he was still under hospital care. I think there were three or four tanks left, and of my ten scout cars there were two.

The battle started with shelling at ten at night. As the scout cars were not being used as targets, we were behind the tanks and I had to remain with two cars together in one place as a marker. In this way anyone could ask me the way to anywhere else or rally back to me from the tanks which were positioned 550 yards in front. No-one could sleep with the din of the shells; they sounded just as other people have said, like trains rumbling along tube tunnels. As the gun flashes were practically constant I could see the line of the front for its whole distance.

We all came under shell fire in our turn but it was intermittent, and with the soldier's abhorrence for unnecessary work, none of us dug a trench. Though there was a pit dug within ten yards of my stand by an Aussie. He was a sapper and worked at night, pulling up enemy mines. He made the hole to try to sleep during the day but said that it was not fair: "How can I sleep with this bloody row?" After the second night he told me he would have to go out the following night as three minefields had been found and they could only tackle one each night. He showed me a white feather he had received from some women in Australia. They had accused him and his mates of dodging the invasion of Australia which they were frightened would be carried out by the Japs. He talked to me of cowardice in general and said that when a shell came near of course your muscles would tremble as it was not natural, but that did not mean the brain was frightened. It was a new way of looking at it.

The next morning an Aussie sergeant came to me and asked: "Has one of my blokes got a hole round here?" I showed him the hole and he told me he was collecting the man's kit. "Is he dead then?" I asked. "Yes, he was blown into a thousand pieces last night," he said. "I picked up a bit of his spine and buried it with his papers." Mines are tricky things and how many nights can one expect to survive?

The battle went on and we stood there. All I had to do was to lend the scout cars out, something like a free taxi service. Once I had to travel somewhere myself with a corporal as a third man. This meant he and I had to stand up as there was only one seat for passengers. There were a few shells coming over but no-one worried about these overmuch. If you heard it, it had not hit you and if you did not hear it, well you would not know. This philosophy was inaccurate but it served its purpose. As we moved a shell burst nearby and coming towards us was a lump of shrapnel the size of a cricket ball. It did

Desert rats

not seem to be going very fast but was humming a little tune to itself. Suddenly the corporal put up his hand to catch it. I knocked his arm sideways, he missed it and looked quite offended. I stopped the car and made him get out with me. There were other bits of shrapnel about and I picked up a piece and showed him the razor sharp edges, made him feel how surprisingly heavy it was, reminded him how hot it would have been while still in the air and told him the piece he had tried to catch would have cut off his arm.

By now some of my cars were gone. They would go out in turn and some would not come back. This one may have hit a mine, that one may have had a direct hit. Most times the men were OK but on one occasion my lieutenant wanted to take a captain of the Royal Engineers on a jaunt to nowhere in particular and he borrowed my own car and the driver. He came back an hour later on foot on his own. I asked him where my car was and he said the captain had wanted to look at something else and would be back in about 20 minutes. An hour later the lieutenant called me to go and look for him. "Follow 'Sun' track," *[see page 72]* he said, "and when you see a group of shot up vehicles on the right, it would be dangerous to take the car farther. From there go on foot."

I followed 'Sun' track and the ground dropped slightly so that the familiar scene of the last few days was out of view, and although we were going forward we seemed to be in quieter country. I saw the burnt out vehicles and stopped the car. There were a few shells coming down but there was nothing definite to fire at and they seemed to be all armour-piercing and did not explode. The ground was quite hard though and the shells did not get buried in the sand, but would break bits of stone which flew around. Suddenly I was the loneliest man in the world. In front, about half a mile away, was a sharp rise in the ground as if it went up a step, and overlooking the crest was a Jerry tank. It was so quiet that I thought it was derelict and carried on walking.

I was still on 'Sun' track and just under the hill the track swung round to the right, or north, in the direction of my regiment. There was a barbed wire fence on the enemy side of the track.

I saw nothing of my car but suddenly a voice from the ground 50 yards to my left said, "Sergeant, what the bloody hell are you doing?" I stopped and it took me a minute to find the owner of the voice. It was an Australian captain in a trench with his troops. I went over to him and he made me get down in the trench. He explained that I would bring fire on him and his men, walking about like that, and wanted to know what I was doing. I told him and with a pair of binoculars he showed me the scout car half a mile along the track from where it turned right. He said that in it was a dead captain of the Royal Engineers.

Desert rats

And a dead tank man. He said, "Your colonel should be satisfied with that if I tell him," and called him up on the radio. He told him what had happened and added that it was far too dangerous for me to go any further, then put me on the line. The colonel seemed to imply I should have gone on but told me to come back.

When I returned my lieutenant seemed to agree with the colonel so I told him I would take him up there. He went without me but he got no further than I did. It was four days later that the bodies were officially identified.

The Aussie captain told me that the tank on the crest had put an 88 shell straight through driver and car. That was the end of my driver; he was 19 years old. I suppose the tank did not want to waste its ammunition on one man so had not fired at me.

Shortly after this my regiment moved forward about a mile, and eight infantrymen rode on the back of each tank. Jerry sent mortar over and they were blown off like flies. There were not so many tanks left now; it was usual when a fighting vehicle is put out of action for it to come back, but none did. Out of action or not though, they stayed at the front. This time they were not to be saved. In fact if the enemy could be induced to expend his arms on useless material, so much the better.

The colonel called a meeting amongst all his fighting officers, who formed a circle under the mortar fire. Next to the colonel stood his sergeant driver, a school master in peacetime. Then the shell landed, the sergeant disappeared and the colonel was so badly wounded that he was finished with the war.

It was at this point that the colonel who had started me up the ladder at last took over the regiment. There was nothing he could do to help the tanks though, which were there to be shot at. As those ten days passed the tanks went out of action. The German Spandeau machine gun was an efficient weapon. Jerry had them fixed six inches above the ground with a traverse of 360 degrees. The ground was being swept by the fire from these guns and as it was night there was not much chance of escape for any on foot. However, the tank wounded were walking back. They generally came to me.

One man, the corporal who had tried to catch the shrapnel, told me he had seen guns with barrels as big as cartwheels and tanks "as high as that", reaching up. I gave him some tea and wrapped him in a blanket till he could go back to base.

A lot of men got back with the help of a little lieutenant. He was very young looking with black curly hair and a chalk white face. In England he had once given us a lecture on map reading (his first I thought). He had told us that in the desert we would have to be most fastidiously pedantic with our maps and cited one instance of a tank commander navigating 50 miles to a bucket on the ground. "He arrived in the dark," he said, "and as he

Desert rats

stepped down, he..." and we added "kicked the bucket".

He still looked the same, as if a cigarette would kill him, but he acquired a jeep and started an ambulance service all by himself. A jeep could not stop an angry fly let alone a bullet, but he went back and forward all that night bringing the men back two at a time. His legs were riddled with bullets from driving that jeep and when we saw him on a visit a year later he was still walking with two sticks.

Near my position were the remains of a barbed wire fence, probably the continuation of the one where my scout car stopped. There was a big gap in it for the vehicles to go forward and this became the busy spot as there were mines each side. As there was no actual road the track became wider and wider as time passed until eventually vehicles could go through four abreast if they felt like it. On about the sixth day a Bren gun carrier had his track blown off by a mine. The driver was very annoyed but he could not have known that he was 30 yards from the original gap.

I saw a complement of the Highland division go through on foot. About 200 of them, led by their pipe major in full regalia playing his pipes. Everyone around watched in silence as we thought there was a lot of 'bull' attached to this mob. Several days later, I suppose when the enemy had retired far too soon, I saw the Highland division come back. The pipe major was still playing and about a dozen men marched behind him. That was all there was left of them. In the meanwhile, somehow they had collected some of their dead and put them in a neat row on the ground by the fence. Later a truck came to collect them, with three men who were efficient at their job. The truck was an open one with a metal floor and walls about two feet high. Two men on the ground each took one end of a corpse and swung it up on the truck. A man on the truck rolled it along in a workmanlike fashion and came back for the next. His two mates kept him busy and he was working very quickly to keep the tail clear.

Then they found an Italian mixed up with their own dead. For a joke they loaded him on as well. The man on the truck was so rushed that he had the poor 'Eyetie' *[slang for Italian]* rolled right up before he realised. The language that followed was terrible and the Eyetie, complete with beard, open eyes and the appearance of still standing to attention, was flung over the side. Well, after all, he had to stack them on top of each other.

The enemy had gone. I was sent on an errand in the dark and was told by an officer that I was in the middle of a minefield, but nothing happened. The battle was over. We listened to the news and thought the war was in its final stages. Jerry was now miles away and hundreds of Italians had come back as prisoners. We knew we would also have to go back.

We had nothing left to speak of and all the squadron

leaders had been killed. And I went back first.

I had not thought about it but we were to have new tanks. The three regiments of the brigade were to be equipped with Shermans and I was sent on a three months' course at Heliopolis *[a suburb of Cairo]* to learn about them.

Within a day of the end of the battle and before I left, we were given bread loaves to eat, the first for months, as the rail had been repaired and a train had come up. It happened to be a coal wagon train. The bread had rolled about the open truck, was as black as coal and as hard. I showed the lads how to wash it and put it in my tin oven: we had the freshest bread.

The three months of the course passed quickly enough. There was one sergeant from each regiment and I met up with Stan once more. He did not know all that much about the subject as he was more of a radio man, so I used to coach him some nights and on others he attended special lectures to catch up. At one of these lectures Stan was amused by a lance corporal who was deputising for the officer instructor. He told me that this man was a Cockney who started the lecture like this:

"Hi 'ave been hasked to take this lecture hin place hof the orficcer 'oo can't be 'ere. Hif there are any questions while the lecture is on you will be placed on a charge for disobeying a horder as all questions will wait till the lecture is hover".

Desert rats

When the lecture was over Stan said he wanted to ask a question but the lance corporal walked straight out.

There was not a great deal of difference between the Sherman and the other tanks. In fact I found that some of the components were the same as those on the tanks we had in peacetime. When I returned to the regiment they already had their complement and did not appear to be waiting for me to tell them how to drive them. However, I had a busy time explaining points. Some of the tanks had diesel and some had petrol engines, and of great interest to me was the fact that the petrol engines were 'two-stroke'. The bigger concern was which tank crew would get a diesel and which a petrol, as, if hit, the petrol ones nearly always went up in flames. The high octane petrol seemed to shock into explosion, but not the diesel ones. In Italy this became a life or death matter.

The regiment was now back at a base camp about five miles west of the pyramids. Here there was a YMCA marquee with many different groups of men using it. There was some trouble between the South Africans and Americans and I do not know how it was resolved. The South Africans looked upon coloured men as if they were slaves but the American negro was dressed in the superior uniform of the American army and drew the same pay as his white comrades. They all wanted to use the YMCA, but South African whites do not use the same places as the blacks and though they stopped their own

Desert rats

blacks, they could not stop the American negroes.

There was one little incident that came to my notice while at this camp. We were still camped on the sand and again used the double tin toilet. One man was very embarrassed while using one. He was sitting there calmly relieving himself when a general's staff car approached. The WAAF (lady) driver pretended not to notice the soldier and with a flourish innocently drove alongside him to stop.

We stayed here for some time. The war had moved to Tunis and when the time came we would be trained and rested, ready to leap-frog into our place in the scheme of things.

An order was published for 'other ranks' who felt like it to apply for commissions, and I gave this a lot of thought. At the time, if a man were commissioned from the ranks half of his service as a ranker would go with his commission. As I had about ten years in, I could be a first lieutenant with five years seniority. There would hardly be an officer in the war with that amount of service in one rank so if I made the grade I would shortly be up in the gods. If one got through the war the cash settlement for an officer was much higher and that was what I was thinking about.

I applied and in due course the colonel sent for me. He told me I was really too old (at 32) and if I passed

Desert rats

out I would go to the Pioneer Corps[1]. He also said that we were going up-desert soon and if I happened to get wounded I would probably be flown to England. On the other hand, to be wounded in some other theatre of war would probably mean I could finish up in Australia. I chose to stay as I was, and he promised to offer me the first sergeant major vacancy that came along.

Shortly after this I was transferred to a troop of tanks as troop sergeant. Even with three stripes it was not automatic that the troop sergeant would take over the troop. There were often other sergeants in a troop and some of them could possibly be senior to the troop sergeant, but while they were on other duties the troop sergeant would take command. Anything concerning the troop was the troop sergeant's job. My friend Frank became scout car sergeant.

My new men and I got used to each other. I found they were efficient and that the gunner knew more about his weapon than I did. I had to do some catching up myself. Eventually the tanks were taken away from us and loaded on to boats for the journey up the Mediterranean. We then got started, travelling right through the desert

---

[1] *The Royal Pioneer Corps was a British Army combatant corps used for light engineering tasks, formed in 1939 and amalgamated into the Royal Logistic Corps in 1993. Pioneer units performed a wide variety of tasks including stretcher-bearing, handling all types of stores, laying prefabricated track on beaches, and effecting various logistical operations.*

The Reservist 181

Desert rats

by truck. It was a leisurely journey and an interesting time. We did about 60 miles a day, about 2,000 all told, and it took about a month. On the way we had a swim each day and plenty of time to camp at night. One day the colonel took us to see the ancient city of Cyrene[1] which had been well preserved, and we stood on the old paved market place. A notice told us to observe the stone lined gullies that cut through the paving and finished in one of the lock-up shops. These were to carry the urine of the populace to the laundry; the laundry advertised that everything was washed in clean water afterwards.

One day we arrived in the vicinity of Sidi-Rezegh and I asked the colonel if I could go there to see if there was a grave for my brother *[Arthur; see p6]*. He was sympathetic but would not let me go. He said he would have taken me if there was anything to see but there was nothing; I would get upset for no purpose. So we went on. We went through or past all the old war zones. None of us had ever been past Alamein before. This is not a travel story and it is not necessary for me to name all the places we passed or went through. The road was difficult as it undulated for most of the way and the bottom of each little descent had been blown up by the retreating

---

[1] *An ancient Greek and Roman city near present-day Shahhat, Libya. It was the oldest and most important of the five Greek cities in the region.*

Desert rats

enemy. This not only prevented speed but caused a detour. This was always hazardous as mines would have been laid each side of the obstruction. Sometimes there had been small bridges over bad bits of ground and these had gone as well. It all slowed progress. In one place near Cyrene a viaduct had gone and our Royal Engineers had made a rough road in its place. There were no accidents though.

One morning I saw a mirage. We were in the habit of moving off at 7.30am and I was watching the column start when I saw a stretch of water in front of it. I knew there was no water there and was interested to discover what happened when the trucks drove through, on or across it. I used my binoculars to see it in more detail and of course the trucks went through without making a ripple on the surface. That was fine, as the water was not there, but they were reflected by the water that did not exist. It was a peculiar sight. It must be unusual for someone to be observing from way back.

Another strange sight was to come across 20 or so miniature tanks which had once belonged to Mussolini. Il Duce[1] had probably regarded them as the secret weapon that would win the war for him. They were made of solid brass and it was a wrench for me to leave them behind

---

[1] *The title assumed by Benito Mussolini, leader of Fascist Italy from 1922 to 1943, and identified as Il Duce, 'The Leader' or literally 'The Duke'.*

when I thought of the price they would fetch as scrap. Each must have weighed a ton. They were about four feet wide, 18 inches high and six feet long, and were designed to hold two men in a prone position side by side: a gunner and a driver. Unless the terrain was like a billiard table the poor devils would not see ten yards in front of them and they were bound to fail. From the way the tanks were scattered around it looked as if the crews might still have been in them.

The Arabs probably picked up these tanks as they seemed to take everything of value, whether it was 'salvage' or not. In Cairo I saw a shop whose stock was all petrol tins. On show at the front was the result of the owner's labour in the shape of saucepans, kettles and so on. All the horse-drawn vehicles in Egypt were shod in Service tyres, in good condition. And when we had a breakdown we had to constantly patrol the car to stop the Arab kids taking anything they could snatch, and we nearly lost the battery from the running board.

I noticed that the beach was all silver sand and I should have liked to collect a few tons. At home ordinary sand was the equivalent of 75 pence for five hundredweight while silver sand was about five pence per pound.

In Cyrenacia[1] we saw Mussolini's colony of one storey

---

[1] *The eastern coastal region of Libya, also known as Pentapolis (Five Cities). It formed part of the Roman province of Crete and Cyrenacia.*

Desert rats

farms geometrically spaced and fenced, all whitewashed, with 'Il Duce' painted on the front in black. It was one of the most ugly places one could imagine, with no facilities for anything, not even a church.

The country was no longer all desert now, and the first free growing fruit we found was the prickly pear. We used our gauntlet gloves as each fruit was covered in half-inch spikes. Even then the spikes pierced through. The natives picked them with a tin fixed to a long pole and since then, at home, I have used the same technique to pick apples from a tree.

One day my crew were picking these things and doing it systematically. Two picked and put the fruit in a rubber bucket, and two peeled, the skin and spikes coming away together. The peeled fruit was going into another bucket, except for those the lads were eating at the same time. Then 'Big Jack' arrived. We called him the 'seagull' because of his habit of taking the leavings from other people's meals.

"What's that you've got lads", he asked. "Prickly pears", said one with his mouth full. "Can I have some?" "Help yourself". Before he could be stopped he had dived into the wrong bucket and it took 20 minutes of holding his mouth open to pluck the spikes from his tongue and the roof of his mouth.

I bought the first oranges I had seen for months from an Arab hawking them for two and a half piastres a

Desert rats

dozen. Then we were introduced to the cicada; we heard its chirping all night and they reminded me of flying fish as they seemed to fly about four feet from the ground; if you were quick you could knock them down from flight. I saw a spider catch one once in its web. It was about four inches long and appeared to be made of ivory with an articulated head and a nice set of teeth. It was trying to eat its way out of the web while the spider made sure the wing tips were secure. Then the spider, about an inch across the body, came to the front and feinting and weaving, tied the cicada's jaws together. It then walked up the body and, testing and finding its ties secure, went to the cicada's shoulder and started eating it.

We saw miles of olive groves, all the trees in straight lines, and I estimated that one crop from the trees we had seen would keep the world in olive oil for ever.

In Tunisia I saw the rifled grave of a Foreign Legion officer. The skeleton was still there in the remains of his greatcoat but the curious thing was that the remains of a snake and a lizard were there as well. The snake had tried to swallow the lizard and it had been too big. Each had suffocated the other.

Italy surrenders

WE HAD a few hours in Tripoli before the last lap of the journey. We picked up our tanks at Medenine[1] and finished at Sfax[2]. I reckoned we had travelled 2,000 miles.

We moved on to Misurata[3] and prepared the tanks for an invasion. This included the fixing of 'fish and chip' shops to the tanks. These were high, flat chimneys to allow the tank to breathe while travelling through water up to six or seven feet deep, and were reminiscent of the old fried fish shops of home. We now knew that we were to take an active part in the invasion of Sicily.

I kept a diary which covers this time:

> "Tuesday, July 20th. Anniversary of first battle when lost tanks on minefield. Embarked at Sousse, town badly damaged, small landing craft. Acted quarter bloke, made 400 cigarettes which shared among troop, also enough tea and sugar for a few brews. Passed Bomb Alley - Lampedusa - Linosota - not one enemy air or sea craft seen in whole voyage."

I realised that the way we were loaded, my tank would be first off the boat and I was hoping that my boat would not necessarily be the first to beach. But it was. When we

---

[1] *The major town in south-eastern Tunisia and the capital of Medenine Governorate.*
[2] *The capital of the Sfax Governorate in Tunisia.*
[3] *A city in the Misrata District in northwestern Libya.*

Italy surrenders

reached the quay my tank drove out and tried to climb on to the stone jetty, but was only managing to push the boat away. With the gap widening, I had to jump off, stop it and let the boat push in again before getting the tank on dry land. This made me the first man of the regiment to set foot on Sicily.

> "Thursday 22nd. Arrived at Syracuse[1], 09.30 hours. Population friendly and waving, town little damage. At moment in lemon and almond groves, two of crew collecting lemons and two almonds. Enjoying themselves like kids in an orchard. Pleasanter country."

To us the country was beautiful and the multiplicity of fruit after the desert was unbelievable. At one stop the colonel sent one lorry from each squadron to a kind of private valley, like the dried bed of a small, swift river. There was a gate at the entrance, guarded by an old Sicilian, and we understood that the fruit inside had been acquired by the NAAFI[2]. We told him we were the NAAFI and he let us in. We picked up tall cane skips and went down the track. In one long plantation were orange,

---

[1] *The capital of the Italian province of Syracuse, located in the southeast corner of Sicily, notable for its rich Greek history.*

[2] *The Navy, Army and Air Force Institutes is an organisation created by the British government in 1921 to run recreational establishments needed by the British Armed Forces, and to sell goods to servicemen and their families.*

Italy surrenders

apple, plum, peach and maybe other fruit trees. I know that within half an hour every skip was full and the floor of each lorry was covered in skips. We drove out and thanked the old man, and the driver of the last truck gave him a receipt, probably signed "T. Atkins[1]".

> *"Saturday, 24th. Tanks go into holding position tomorrow, crew quite happy."*
> *"Sunday, 25th. Taken out of tank to make room for new officer who requires battle experience - tanks move out - Mussolini packs up."*

I now went into 'B' echelon, the truck section that ferried food and ammunition to the tanks. This was strange ground to me and I knew no-one. As I was only 'attached' I was really a spectator and passenger and, as such, was in a unique position to see how the echelon was run. This was in such a fantastic way that if I had invented it, a reader would say, "How stupid to think that we could swallow that this happened in wartime." I saw it happen.

The 'B' echelon, not a fighting unit but very necessary, was made up of soft-skinned vehicles. It was always several miles behind the hard-skinned fighting vehicles ('A' echelon) and its job was to keep them supplied with food, ammunition and water. It received these from other

---

[1] *Tommy Atkins is slang for a common soldier in the British Army, often just shortened to 'Tommy'. It was particularly associated with World War I.*

Italy surrenders

trucks from base, and this was left to the major in charge. The colonel had enough to do in the front line and would very seldom leave his tank or staff car to go back to his 'B' echelon.

Water was still rationed and we all had mosquito-netted tents. The major had a bed pitched at the side of a large open space. It had four posts at the corners which held netting draped round and over the top. There was enough room at the side for a large canvas bath.

The unit paraded at eight in the morning and they formed up facing the bed in which the major was still lying. The sergeant major took the parade and marched up to the bed, saluted and reported. The major waved his hand and told him to carry on. The sergeant major then returned to the parade and dispersed the men. Watching this I was stupified but it had not yet ended. The major called his orderly to fill his bath from several water cans, and as this was being carried out he objected that the water was over chlorinated and discoloured. The orderly had to find the tanker and get more water before the major rose.

The corporal driver of my truck told me that this performance occurred every day. I wondered why the sergeant major put up with it and could only think he was hanging on to a 'safe' job. But news reached the colonel; three days later he was watching, unseen and seething with rage. That major was gone in an hour, back to base,

Italy surrenders

where if he retained any rank at all he would never get any higher. I wondered how he got his promotion in the first place.

Three miles away his regiment's tanks were in action.

For several days I had been riding on the corporal's truck up to the tanks and back. We had been taking ammunition up, and a most unpleasant job it was. The tanks were positioned close to an escarpment and

Jerry could not hit them with shells but he tried hard with mortar and a new kind of rocket. On impact this made an intense fire and woe betide anything which was within 20 yards of the impact point. I did not like it when these things were dropping while we were carefully giving out supplies.

On my first of these trips the corporal stopped at a place where the road went over the top of a hill. He said Jerry had this place ranged and we would stay there till the firing stopped. Jerry fired at regular intervals and we waited for the next lull. On the left of the road at this point was the remains of a truck that had received a direct hit, which proved the point about Jerry having the range. On the right of the road was a circular silo pit, machine cut and about 10 yards in diameter and 12 feet deep. While we waited we looked into this pit. In the centre was a spike of rock sticking up about four feet and as the cutting machine had gone round it, it had tapered to a point. And that's where the truck driver was. He had

Italy surrenders

been blown out of the truck across the road into the pit and onto the spike. He lay in bits round the spike's base. Next time we passed and waited, someone had piled earth over the place and put a cross there.

That day was the last of that action and I think the last contact we had with the enemy in Sicily. One man had climbed the escarpment in the night to find Jerry had pulled out. He climbed down with a portable gramophone and a record which he proudly played. That was the first time we heard 'Lili Marlene'[1].

That night we heard the dumps in Catania being blown up. Timing the flashes to the bangs[2] we estimated we were 20 miles away. We could plainly see the tracer from the ack-ack and it was surprising to notice the way the nearly spent bullets wandered across the sky. We could see the same little lights going to and fro, to and fro, till finally disappearing.

> "August 4th. Lorries moved up to where I refuelled tanks Monday. Jerry gone miles back. Sent back for new tank Wednesday but not arrived. Brought back grapes and was ill from arsenic wash."
>
> "August 5th. Again went for tank and again not arrived. Heard Catania was full of dead."

[1] *'Lili Marlene'*, originally a poem set to music by a German composer, was a popular song between 1941 and 1945, representing a shared longing for peace. Marlene Dietrich was best known for singing it.

[2] *Counting the number of seconds between the flash of light and the sound of the explosion.*

Italy surrenders

Except for a note in my diary to the effect that I could not write home as I had no money nor stamps, things fell back into a normal routine. The squadron leader told me we were eight drivers short and asked if I thought I could get some men trained by the end of 10 days. It was a relief to get back to things I knew about, but I nearly slipped up teaching men to drive tanks on the terrain of Sicily.

Another thing against the job was that the mechanics were different. On the old tanks, when steering, a lever was pulled which put a positive brake on the track, on the side selected; then it stopped dead and the tank spun on its centre till the lever was released. On these new Shermans all that happened when the lever was pulled was a change to a very low gear. To make an emergency stop on the old type you pulled both levers on at once, but when that was done on the Sherman, the thing still went on, albeit very slowly. Although all tanks had a foot brake it could not stop the weight like the two levers did.

So I conducted the lesson up a mountain, a nice grass-sloped one, and over the top. About eight men as well as me were on the front of the tank. I was nearest the learner driver. We started the descent and to my horror I realised that the Sicilians had 'stepped' this side for cultivation purposes. The slope was still steep but every ten yards was a step of two feet and the angle would

Italy surrenders

turn the tank over. I shouted "All off!" and the riders were off like a flock of sparrows. I gave quick instructions to the driver: "Grip both sticks, pull as hard as you can and if it goes over, switch off."

Then I joined the other sparrows. The tank inexorably crept on. It reached the step and its own weight saved it. If the terrain had been rock, at that angle to start with, it would have gone on over the edge till the point of balance was reached, the front would have dipped and nothing could have saved it from rolling right over. Having started rolling, it might have kept on. As it was, the tracks cut through the step and although the nose of each track hit the ground, that actually helped to stop it. I changed the route but it had been a hard job to see those steps from the top.

On Saturday, 21st August 1943, the regiment took a trip to Mount Etna. It was to be a kind of holiday climb. Nobody troubled to tell us where we were going, and my first view of the volcano gave me something to remember. We drove round a hill and I saw a field in the sky; a green field with clouds below it. Other clouds obscured everything else. It was only when we approached much closer that I realised I had been looking at a higher slope of Etna. It was the last approach slope before the cone itself and the heat had kept it lush and green. My diary states:

"Arrived at Etna Hotel, camped outside for the night

Italy surrenders

as it was 'officers only'. Found it cold."

On Sunday morning we travelled two more miles by truck to the lower observatory. Then there was a six mile climb. The diary entry reads:

"Started at 8am. Arrived top at 12.30 on knees."

I remember one long slope that seemed to take hours. I had the squadron clerk for a companion. He needed the exercise and I had bad varicose veins. We staggered up a few yards at a time and rested. While we were resting, the lads would come tripping lightly down, wave "Hello, Sarge" and trip lightly on. They were making it there and back in two and a half hours. But many did not make it at all.

We eventually walked across that field I had seen in the sky. The ground was warm and had little jets of steam spurting from it. The cone looked about 1,000 feet straight up. I looked at my mate. I do not like heights and get giddy on a ten feet ladder. He had guts, that clerk. He was not as fit as me but he said, 'We have come so far, Sarge." So we started on the cone. It was like warm, soft coke, and we kicked a foothold and went up. Somehow it seemed easier than it looked and the height did not affect me. But the result of it all was disappointing. The view across to Italy was hidden from the crater by mist. Only one small corner of the crater was active and that sounded like a huge bowl of porridge being stirred.

Italy surrenders

On reaching base again I was met by an officer.

"Sergeant, did you reach the top?"

"Yes, sir."

"Bugger you," he said, "You lost me a bet."

With my remaining strength I gave him an unsympathetic laugh.

While in Sicily and later in Italy, we had men rejoin us who had been wounded at Alamein, or had just been left behind with some lesser complaint. These men had been left in Cairo and some had even been sent back to Palestine. Every troop movement was top secret; we had moved 2,000 miles up the desert, crossed a sea and then got lost in a new country, and yet these men, though not many, found us.

Men left behind like this would be sent to a 'holding' unit on leaving hospital and the system knocked the *esprit de corps* out of the army, if it was allowed to do so. As a batch of men became available, they could be sent to where they were needed, wherever that was, and that meant saying goodbye to their mates and the regiment that they were becoming proud to belong to.

The result was that the men deserted. I think a lot of eyes were shut to it. The deserters then hitch-hiked by plane, sea or truck, 2,000 to 3,000 miles. They did not know where they were going, except in the general direction of the front where their mates might be. When they got within 100 miles, they would just ride around

Italy surrenders

looking for tanks and would eventually report in as if it were the most natural thing in the world.

We stayed on in Sicily till September and embarked for Italy on Tuesday 21st, sailing at 7.30 the next morning and arriving at Taranto on Thursday afternoon. Half the Italian fleet seemed to have been sunk in the harbour and in a very convenient manner: all round the edge. So it would have been easy for them to walk off deck on to land as the ship grounded, and probably also easy to rescue personal effects before they got wet. All the boats had their funnels out of the water and they looked as if they had just been lowered gently down. There was no sign of the enemy but we heard that the Front was 25 miles away.

On Monday I was able to go on a trip into town from our camp, accompanied by Frank. We sampled the cherry brandy and decided it was made of almonds, but there was not much to do or see there.

We were told that we were to be in position by October 1st and I saw to it that my drivers were passed out. The colonel decided I could now have a break. On Thursday 30th we packed up everything and moved down to the docks and at 2pm on Friday we sailed for an unknown destination. By first light on Saturday we were back in Taranto with a newly arrived convoy. We sailed in the direction of Bari round the 'heel'.

Sunday, 3rd October: my birthday once more, the fifth

Italy surrenders

of the war and, as it was raining and cold, it reminded me of the first one, when we leaned each side of the haystack at St. Nazaire.

We sighted Brindisi at 1pm and we were well escorted. On Monday we stopped at Candia and disembarked, expecting to travel in the direction of Foggia. We made several preliminary moves and on the next Saturday we moved into the second line with one squadron forward. On Sunday we backed the tanks into a wood. This was all dead secret. The tracks were to be erased when the tanks were hidden. While I was getting my tank in, standing in front of it, a Jerry plane very unkindly swooped down and fired a burst at it. He hit it several times and I wondered how his bullets had missed me, as I was standing between him and the tank. I did not now see the point of erasing our tracks but we did it just the same. This was just by Termoli.

Being on the winning side in an action means that the arena is in your hands and the whys and wherefores of various aspects can be studied with the facts in sight.

On Monday 11th, the colonel took the officers and tank sergeants to the scene of a recent action by a sister unit. The immobilised tanks were still in their battle positions and the crews were still in them, the dead ones that is. The colonel gave us the lesson of the battlefield. On the same jaunt we saw the new 17 pounder gun which was reckoned to be the answer to the Jerry 88, four years

Italy surrenders

from when that gun drove us through Dunkirk.

We also saw pigs from a farm rooting through the newly-made graves and could do nothing to stop them. We could not shoot all the pigs, nor put a wall round the graves which had been dug where the occupants had fallen, and were therefore scattered.

On Wednesday we went to reconnoitre a town we were destined to attack. It did not look good tank ground to me and I was relieved to find that our patrols were already in it.

We now learned that the Italians had declared war on Germany[1]. What a country! We saw the Eyeties getting back into the uniforms they had hidden when they had deserted. I supposed that when we gave an armistice they would also.

> *"Friday 15th: Learned that 'C' Squadron had taken Pettaciatto so we still seem to be in business."*
> *"Saturday 16th: Had a bath at a mobile unit and was issued with winter clothing."*
> *"Sunday 17th: Carried out the army commandment: 'Six days shalt thou labour and on the seventh do*

---

[1] *In the summer of 1943, as Allied forces landed in Sicily, public support for the war and for Mussolini diminished. Mussolini was ousted on July 25th and his replacement, General Pietro Badoglio, sought peace with the Allies, and reached an armistice on September 3rd. Italy surrendered to the Allies in October 1943, then declared war on Nazi Germany, its one time Axis powers partner.*

Italy surrenders

all thy odd jobs.' Sewed stripes on winter battle dress, did washing, wrote home."

Now we had a week of waiting, and as we knew that we should soon be in the thick of it again it was a hard time to pass away. The weather was wet and cold, the country looked cheerless although picturesque. All the villages seemed to be built on the top of near mountains. One day I was frightened out of my wits by the first Auster[1] plane I had ever seen. I heard the noise of a motorcycle engine above me, very near, coming from my rear. Suddenly it swooped down at a steep angle and landed under a tree in front. The pilot jumped out, covered it with a camouflage net and walked away. The thing had not needed a runway. When the wheels touched down, the tail dropped and there it was, parked. When a little later the pilot flew off, he just seemed to lift it at 45 degrees, straight up and away. He flew from our hilltop to a similar one across the valley in a couple of minutes. It would have taken a jeep an hour.

We were to attack a village called San Salvo which was across the Trigno River. We took a waiting position in a valley. The Trigno was over the ridge and down the next valley. From the other side of the river the ground rose gradually for about a mile and then steeply up to a village

[1] The Taylorcraft Auster was a British light aircraft used in large numbers by the RAF for artillery spotting and communications duties.

Italy surrenders

we could see on the crest. It looked deserted and the church appeared to be a ruin but the bell still pealed at the proper times.

We waited in our valley for two days and the rain kept on. I noticed that the trees had no leaves and realised this was because of the effect of the shrapnel shells the enemy kept sending over. Perhaps the time in the desert had made me unaccustomed to trees but it did not strike me till the shrapnel came, and it kept on for the two days. Each tank crew sat close to one side of their tank and the shrapnel hit the other. The only drawback was that, as sergeant, I had to break cover to draw rations, as did the other troop sergeants.

During this wait I thought it silly and wrong to have a church parade on Sunday; the padre called everyone together under the quite persistent rain of shrapnel. On top of this, the theme of his sermon was, "You may not be here for much longer, so make your peace now." It certainly did nothing to boost the morale of 20-year-old men who had been waiting 24 hours under fire to make an attack. Still, no-one was hurt physically.

The continual rain was no help to the tanks as we would have to ford the river and drive across the approach on low ground to it beforehand. We started In the pre-dawn dark of Tuesday and knocked out the first defence of the enemy: the machine guns on the way to the river. And here I have to go back 24 hours.

Italy surrenders

I said that when I was transferred back to the tanks my crew knew more than I did about the working of them. I still had the same crew, I was in practice again, and the very fact that I had had to work to catch up with my crew had made them one of the best trained in the unit. I had been lucky in getting a good crew to start with and then being able to give them more training while I got in training myself. The day before we actually started the San Salvo attack, the squadron leader approached me.

"Sergeant," he said, "You have a good crew and I am going to reward them. I am making three of them lance corporals." I was pleased for the men and thanked him. An hour later a message came to me that there could not be one sergeant and three lance corporals on one tank and therefore the squadron leader would take my driver, and my gunner would go to another officer's tank.

So I went into action with a good lorry driver who had never driven a tank with the driving flap down (which meant he had to drive using a periscope) and a gunner whose capabilities I knew nothing about and it was too late to do anything.

So we drove over the soft, rained-on approach to the river and the tank became bogged. Two other tanks were bogged as well and we could not get out. We were hampered by a sniper who kept at us but I was not pulled out till ten in the morning by the adjutant as he came up. This made me late to take up my position

Italy surrenders

across the river and as I approached I could see a Jerry tank coming forward and taking up position.

I stopped to watch him as he unloaded a machine gun, mounted it on a tripod and set it up beside the tank. I radioed the colonel, giving the Jerry's position, which was to the right of the regiment. The colonel could not see it from where he was, and I suggested I put a shot at it. He vetoed this as I was still at the rear of the unit, and he may not have liked the idea of my sending one of our low trajectory shells so near our own men. But he told me to take up position to the right of the regiment as my normal place had been filled. I went to the right and knew I would be coming more or less head on to my Jerry.

At the end of the field I crossed a two foot step into the next field, and at this time Jerry was out of sight. My driver, with his visor down and looking through the periscope, could not negotiate the step. I had not thought this would be an obstacle, as both my old driver and I could have made it even if it had meant slewing sideways and halving the angle, as a horse does on a hill. The tank stood reared up and helpless with the driver saying, "I can't make it, Sarge." As I was saying "Reverse", the first shell hit us. Across the front of the tank a piece of armour plating had been spot-welded to repair some old damage, and there was a horrible clanging noise as the impact of the shell broke the plating away and it went sailing over my head. I estimated that

Italy surrenders

that plate weighed two hundredweight and it missed me by a foot. The driver said he could not reverse, and the shell had lodged in the gear box. It was marvellous shooting but better was to come. I said, "Depress the gun," because although only seconds had elapsed, the gun was still parallel with the tank, and therefore pointing at the sky. As I spoke the next shell hit us and the gunner said, "I can't move it." That second shell had gone under the gun, between the trunnions[1] and had wedged it.

The tank was helpless so I ordered the men out. There were three turrets, the main one from which I was looking, and a smaller one each side at the front for the driver and co-driver. I had to jump first followed by the gunner and radio man, while the driver and his mate got out of their places. We were in an apple orchard and as my gunner jumped he said he had been hit. The driver got out but the co-driver had been hit and could not get out without help. I told the two who were unhurt to get back behind one of the trees which were about a foot thick, and I went with them. We had gone back 50 yards and the ground between the trees had been ploughed and was corrugated. I then realised that the gunner who had said he was hit was still lying where he had landed when he jumped. I went back for him. We were still under fire; Jerry was not only trying to set the tank on fire, he

[1] *Two opposing projections on which a gun barrel can be tilted vertically.*

Italy surrenders

was trying to stop us getting near it.

I got hold of the gunner under his armpits and pulled him over the first corrugation. He said, "Thanks very much". I pulled him over the second. He said "Thanks very much". After about the fifth repeat I said, "Shut up for Christ's sake", and put him in line behind the tree. We were one behind the other in a line. I had not noticed that when hitting a tree the shells went straight on snapping the tree off as if cut by a saw.

Then I and one of the others went back for the co-driver. We lifted him out, and I will say that though we must have been within full view of the Jerry crew, the same one I had seen at the beginning, they let us get that man out before firing again. My tank was a diesel and it just stood there. They put 11 shells in it before leaving it; they had to then as the battle had started in earnest.

We lay there in the middle of the apple orchard all day. We were in the middle of a tank battle and were strafed and dive-bombed three times by the British and twice by the enemy.

This is when I noticed the superior design of the Jerry tank. The foliage in an orchard is quite low. The Sherman was tall and the tank commander's view was screened. The opponents' Tiger tanks were low and the commanders could look straight down the avenues, wait till an opposing tank drove across and kill it from almost point blank range.

Italy surrenders

We saw this happen several times while one Jerry was in position 50 yards from us. We also saw the difference between the petrol and diesel tanks of our own side. One hit on a petrol tank and the impact seemed to explode it, and a sheet of flame would come up through the turret enveloping the commander, and his body would block his crew from escaping. To my mind Jerry won, but with most of these fluid battles both sides pull back, and that is what happened in this case.

Meanwhile, we took advantage of the shift in the conflict and went back to the tank for our personal possessions and I discovered a curious thing. Tank commanders had been told that as the 'issue' binoculars should always be hanging round the neck, if they were lost the commander would pay for them. I thought I had lost mine but they were on the ground where I had jumped. I picked them up and, although I had just lost a £20,000 vehicle, I was relieved to find them. The neck strap, which was only a quarter of an inch thick, had been neatly cut in half by a bullet. Trying to work it out, I decided that the gunner with the tripod had opened up when I jumped. One of his first bullets had hit that strap as it swung away from me when I jumped. His next effort had caught the second man fair and square: I learned later that the man who had kept thanking me had 12 bullets and a piece of shrapnel in him. As he was just over five feet tall I do not think he could have held many

Italy surrenders

more, but the amount of lead in him may have accounted for his weight when I pulled him. (I happened to meet him back in England; he was active, well and happy.)

And now I come to the awkward part. I had to leave a man behind. The co-driver was badly hurt. He was a student doctor and knew more about his condition than I did. I was taking the other three back in the moonlight. For all his wounds the gunner could walk with help; the other man could not. We could hear our tanks in the distance revving up about three miles away as they positioned for the night, but Jerry had positioned his tanks between us and our own. He had put them in triangular formation and every so often a burst of machine gun fire would come from one or the other, firing into the open. The moon was bright and I did not see how I could move that man. I offered him morphia [*morphine*] which I carried, but he refused it. I did not like the idea of trying to carry him. Apart from the extra burden of him as well as the other man I thought I would do him more harm trying to carry him that distance. Something I had learned when working for London Transport came back to me. I had been taught that even if a bus wheel was standing on someone, it was better to leave it there than to drive off. Either you made the already damaged place irreparable or you damaged something else. I thought that leaving him where he was he might recover; humped somehow across three

Italy surrenders

miles of country, regularly putting him down for rests, he was less likely to last. He was not bleeding and I made him comfortable as far as I could, leaving him water and cigarettes. We left him wrapped in all our blankets. I still do not know if I should have stayed. I know that he was picked up next day and taken to hospital but I don't know whether he got through or not.

We started back and I made the men leave behind anything that glinted, such as mess tins. The enemy tanks were about 100 yards apart and we walked between them. Without saying a word and walking as softly as we could, we went past them and towards where we could still hear our own tanks now and again in the distance. The strain told. Perhaps as an older man it hit me harder. This was the second night without any sleep and before that we had not had much either in that waiting period under the shrapnel fire. We were walking through open fields but we came to a few trees grouped together and I could see a German sniper lying along the branch of one of them. I stopped the others and we froze for five minutes till we could see that he was no longer there.

We went on across the next field where there was a hedge about 500 yards away; behind that would be our tanks. I saw a small party of men in front of that hedge walking from right to left: an enemy patrol, I thought. I stopped the men and told them to stand still. We stood in the moonlight and the patrol got down to the ground.

Italy surrenders

"Stay still," I said, "they are taking up firing positions." They got up again and moved on. So did we until they stopped again. I stopped my men and that patrol once more went down. We froze till they moved and at last reached our own lines. I reported the 'patrol' and was told it was a stretcher party bringing in a wounded man. Every so often they had rested and all squatted down, then went on.

In the morning the enemy had retired, presumably to straighten their line, as our other squadrons had also crossed the river and taken their objectives. My squadron had lost 13 of its 16 tanks and, though the advance was maintained, we just followed on. My proper driver, the one appointed lance corporal, was killed while driving the major's tank. His mates told me that they had buried him at the foot of a wall round a farm. Two women who still lived at the farm had come out later and dug him up plus a couple of others. They wanted them taken from the proximity of the farm, and the lads had to comply. If they had acted differently the graves would have been opened again. When I heard this I remembered this young man in the desert: he and I had once looked over one of our tanks that had been put out of action. On what had been the driver's seat was a stump of burned flesh going up to a point. The man had burned like a candle. My driver had said, "I don't want to finish like that". I told him not to get morbid and led him away. He was only 19 then. He had

Italy surrenders

died more or less in the same way.

I thought I had been served a dirty trick when my crew had been split up at the last minute and the best men taken from me. In the long run maybe that is why I am still here. My good driver would not have got caught in the marsh to start with. We would therefore have been in the thick of the battle, not at the side of it.

All this took its toll. After this action I went down with an outbreak of boils. I was not able to work with these things covering my arms and hands, they were even on the backs of my fingers. In any case I had no tank now. I now realise that this was probably a nervous reaction. This was when I learned that the man whom I had left behind had been picked up and, according to my diary, *"was okay"*.

A week later, as the regiment was investigating the crossing of the next river, the Sangro, we were pulled out and went across to the vicinity of Naples, to comparative

Wally's tank crew in Tunisia (Wally is in the middle). Three were made lieutenant corporals and taken away from him. The man kneeling on the left was the one who was hit by several bullets. The one kneeling on the right was taken away to drive the major's tank and was killed, to be buried twice.

Italy surrenders

quiet. As I was still sick, a younger sergeant had taken over my troop and I was travelling on a truck. The tank crews were getting four days leave in Naples but I would have to wait as I was no longer one of the elite.

Before we had quite settled we camped in Cirio's jam factory at Mondragone for a night from where we could see our warships shelling the next town along the coast. The factory was completely smashed up and there were stacks of crates of tomato ketchup everywhere. Every truck and tank took on a few crates but everyone forgot that the cooks would do the same, and for days afterwards every meal served by the cookhouse had this stuff on it somewhere. We got sick of the sight of it and most of what the lads had taken was thrown away.

I was sent on a temporary job to Naples as sergeants' mess caterer to the 'holiday camp'. The camp was actually the workhouse and the male inmates still lived there. We had the top floor while they had the lower. Our cooks used to throw the swill porridge from a back window and we saw the ground-floor tenants come out, scrape it up with their hands and eat it. The cooks took it away after that.

My pal Frank came on leave and we went out together on the town. I had been told that Napoli was the biggest slum in Europe and that walk around seemed to prove it. Sailing into the bay, the colours of the houses had looked beautiful but on closer inspection the peeling

Italy surrenders

paint and colour washes, and the general deterioration of the buildings made us feel that if we entered a place, it would be advisable to be de-loused on coming out. We did go in an arcade off the Via Roma and I bought a little china horse. I sent it to my wife with a note to the effect that I was hanging on its tail.

This was the middle of December and I had not the faintest idea that I would be back in England in less than three months.

❈ ❈ ❈

Back to Blighty[1]

I RETURNED to the regiment on the 14th and in my diary I see that I:

"shook up the RSM of the holiday camp when I showed him how wide open the books were."

With big money I expect I would be as dishonest as the next, but I have no interest in little 'fiddles'.

On return to duty I had a talk with my squadron major. He told me I was too old to go back in the tanks again, and said that if I liked I could ride about on a truck until the end of the war. We had other 'passengers' like this and I was not going to be one of them. He then told me something I had never realised. Following the regiment at a safe distance was its driving and maintenance school, and he asked if I would like to try instructing there. All this time this little peacetime unit had been following along. I had not much choice; I had to go somewhere and I said I would try it.

The next day I said goodbye to my mates and, with all my kit, was taken back about seven miles to the 'D&M' school. It was situated in a large private house in its own

---

[1] A slang term first used during the Boer War to mean homeland for the English or British. It was used in India during the 1800s to mean an English or British visitor. According to The Oxford English Dictionary the word derives from "bilayati", a regional variant of the Hindi word "vilayati", meaning 'foreign', 'British', 'English' or 'European'.

Back to Blighty

grounds; it had a sign up to say what it was. There I met a captain whom I had not seen since we left England. He had been in charge of D&M then, and still was. He sat at his desk and I stood in front of it. He gave me a syllabus of the curriculum and I studied it. He then called in Sergeant G and told me that if I needed help Sergeant G would be pleased to give it. The last time I had seen this sergeant was in England and he had been on that first tank course the colonel had sent me on when he promoted me. I had passed the course 'QI' and he had scraped through with a '2'. He had kept his notebooks but mine had been destroyed in case they fell into enemy hands. He beamed at me and I felt my temper rising. I looked at the syllabus: 'carburation, four hours', and I told the captain a few things that I might not have done had I been feeling normal.

"Carburation when they have diesel tanks! I would sooner talk to them for four hours on this pipe (producing mine). Why don't you teach them to drive with the visor down instead of this rubbish."

He went red with rage but I could shout as loud as him, and I told him I was returning to the regiment.

He said, "You are confined to the camp", and I laughed at him.

I picked up my kit which was where I had dumped it and was approached by a trooper. He must have been keyholing and was on my side.

Back to Blighty

"Sarge, wait till 12 o'clock," he said. "The medical officer is coming and he will give you a lift back."

I thanked him and waited. When the medical officer arrived he had the colonel with him. The D&M captain did not know how well the colonel knew me. I was waiting outside the front door to catch the medical officer and the captain came to the door to greet him. On seeing the colonel with him he thought he would get one back at me and, with a bright smile, said,

"Oh sergeant, you wanted to see the colonel didn't you?" The colonel swung round to face me, recognised me then got out of the jeep.

He came over and said, "What's the matter, Harmer?"

I told him I could not teach this stuff, and that I did not relish the idea of being a passenger for the rest of the war. My nerves were in such a state that I broke down while talking to him. I then told him that if I was now no good at my old job, I would go in as a trooper and he could take back the stripes.

He said, "I know what's wrong with you; I have been flogging a willing horse. You will see a psychiatrist and will come back to the regiment with me."

The next day I was told a truck would take me to the psychiatrist for 8am and I was to be ready at 7.30am. The journey was several miles and the consulting room was a marquee. There were others waiting outside and it looked as if I would have a long wait. Then my colonel

Back to Blighty

came out of the marquee, looked at me and was driven away. I went in next. The colonel had made an effort to get there before me although it was quite a distance.

The doctor looked at me and said, "Sergeant, you are very ill and you are going back *[home]*." Strangely, I objected and said I felt fine but he took no notice. I went back to the regiment, collected my kit and just had time to find Frank and say goodbye before leaving the regiment for good. I saw the colonel once more before leaving; he said he had recommended me for a training unit in England. He shook hands and said he had never regretted promoting me.

I was taken to the 2nd General Hospital in Naples. The boils on my arms were bad; they were bandaged up and I was not allowed to write. I was a bed patient at Christmas and the nurses and doctors put on a nice little show of carol singing with violin accompaniment which was very effective in the stone passages of the place. For years after, 'Silent night' brought back that place to me.

I had been in hospital in the peacetime army and had had a set-to with an officious, fat orderly. There was a similar type in this place. I thought he was the same man and felt like having a go at him. I was classed as a dangerous patient and on the night of the 26th my bed was pushed down to outside the office of the night sister. At 4am I was told to get up, and at 5am I was down on the dock waiting to be picked up by a hospital ship. It

Back to Blighty

was a cold, miserable morning, and my wife's birthday. While I waited I could not help noticing the art that had gone into making the customs man's office bomb proof. It was a kiosk made of concrete, perfectly circular and domed. The dome did not quite finish but went up symmetrically about another six feet to a point. There was no place where it could receive a direct hit.

I boarded the boat and sailed for Africa. One of the people I met was Franz, a German prisoner, who was also a sergeant and had the freedom of the ship. I was told his brain had been turned by an encounter with Ghurkas when most of his troop had had their throats slit; but he seemed normal and I played a game of chess with him. Suddenly he gave a yell and jumped over some railings straight down to the next deck. He had seen a coloured man and that had brought it all back.

We arrived at Phillipville on December 29th and disembarked on the 30th. We were at 67 General Hospital Sand once more and the weather was bleak. I was seen by various doctors and told I would be going home. I was also told not to tell other patients as there were quite a few malingerers. On New Year's Day the wind ripped the roof from the marquee which was my ward, and it was a morning's work for the staff to get it on again while we inmates tried to keep the cold rain off the bed patients. It passed the time away as there was absolutely nothing to do except sit on the bed all day. I

Back to Blighty

was glad to get out of there and to be sent to a holding camp within some 200 miles of Algiers.

The camp consisted of wooden huts erected alongside a railway line that, as far as I knew, was the continuation of the line from Alamein a couple of thousand miles back. One day I was told to take charge of a party of 12 men who were going home. I was given numerous instructions: rations to draw, reveille at 4am, to catch the Rapido train and so on. I did not think it was much more than 100 miles to Algiers and was surprised at the quantity of food we were given. It was contained in a large wooden box with rope handles, and it was all two men could do to carry it. The Rapido train went from a station about 30 miles in the wrong direction; we boarded our lorry and started at 5am.

We found the Rapido and saw that it was the usual horse-box, cement floor type, and then I noticed that other passengers were gathering bricks. I told my lot to get some as well though I did not know yet for what. We took a carriage to ourselves and saw a tin with holes in left by the last victims; then we realised what the bricks were for. Using them as a stand and the crate as firewood, the tin became a fireplace to cook the grub on. Outside the door of each coach was a nail to hang the brazier on to fan the flames. An hour after we started, the train stopped for a 30 minute rest, outside the camp we had left. We saw the men going to breakfast and waited till they came out again. If we had known we could have joined them; we need not have done that journey at all. We had been travelling since 4am and we were back where we started.

The Rapido travelled on and the pace was such that when tea was required, one man got off, caught up with the engine, pointed to his receptacle and the driver obligingly pulled a lever and filled it with boiling water. When the carriage caught up with him, as the tea was already made, it could be poured. The brazier was kept for soup.

It took the Rapido 36 hours to reach Algiers. It seemed to stop every 20 miles or so for a rest or maybe the engine was required for shunting purposes. When it stopped the wait was at least 20 minutes and each time it stopped a funny thing happened. There seemed to be, in the words of that lieutenant I had met, miles and miles of sweet FA [*nothing*] and yet, out of the sand rose hordes of Arabs. One minute the train was chugging along at a steady eight miles per hour and the countryside was desolate and deserted. Then it stopped and immediately the Arabs were alongside in their flowing robes, bargaining for anything the lads would sell them. There was nothing to worry the lads, no check on kit, and when our destination was reached, they could just say, "Kit lost in action," and be issued with a new lot. The things sold were fantastic. I saw one man sell the

Back to Blighty

boots he was wearing and an officer sell his greatcoat. The transactions were carried out in an atmosphere of mutual distrust, the Arab counting out half the price and taking one boot and then the same for the second one. At the end of the deal if the buyer could delay things long enough for the train to start off once more he would wave the vendor goodbye and forget to finish paying. Similarly, if the vendor could see his chance just before the train got under way, he would snatch back the goods he had just sold, to sell again at the next stop. I saw deals being completed with the Arab running with the train for 200 yards, counting out money while keeping one hand on his purchase. All these Arabs had big wads of English notes.

We arrived at Algiers and, following the instructions I had been given, we made for a sports field which had been converted into a transit camp. We arrived with our still heavy box of food. The usual set-up confronted us: a running track round the perimeter and grass in the centre. Opposite the entrance was what used to be a kiosk. Now it was labelled 'Inquiries'. The whole field was covered with little two-men tents and big ration crates like ours.

In the kiosk was a cockney lance corporal. He was one of those men who, although having gained the first step, did not have any time for anyone higher, or lower for that matter.

Back to Blighty

"You came here looking for a boat, Sarge," he said, "you don't want to stay in this bleeding dump. Look at them all, been here for bleeding weeks. If you want to get away go to so and so, it's only half a mile away."

I took his advice and followed his directions and shortly after we arrived at a similar place where we put our box down and looked around. We were looking for some kind of shelter as we had no tents and, having decided that we were going to be unlucky, came across a blackboard and easel (just like the day I came off Reserve).

The message informed everyone that men who were due to sail had to parade that night at 10 o'clock in full marching order.

We all paraded and there was a long line of trucks with a set of steps to mount and fitted out with forms to sit on. A military policeman shepherded us on, no-one asked to see any papers, and off we went. We sailed in the morning. I was glad of the lance corporal's advice.

During that three weeks voyage back to Blighty I gave up smoking. I knew that tobacco was much dearer at home and thought I had better get used to going without. But my first buy on reaching England was an ounce of tobacco.

We sighted the coast of Ireland 36 hours before we docked at Liverpool. Everyone rushed down and packed his kit and then we lined the deck rail throughout that miserable day, watching the line of the low hill coast go

Back to Blighty

past till it was too dark to see it. We docked the next day.

Throughout my time in Africa I had been corresponding with my pal Frank's parents and as most of us were going to Catterick the next day, I thought I would visit them while I had a chance. Knowing the address by heart, I set out to find it. Eventually I knocked at the door and it was opened by Frank's mother. She had never seen me, nor had a photograph, but I had the Eighth Army medal ribbon on my uniform and I thought that as an army mother she would know that I had just come back.

Her reception dumbfounded me. She told me to clear off. She "did not want my type coming here". I did not know what to say except that I had been writing to her. She would not have it, so I turned away and had gone quite a way before something must have clicked and she called to me. I very nearly walked on but thought of Frank and went back. After that it was okay and she and Frank's father, and later his invalid brother, made me very welcome.

It seemed a pity that most of the lads who lived in or near Liverpool had to go to Catterick before they could have the leave they were due. As for me, my wife was in Middlesbrough and it was all on the way.

I had one nasty little experience travelling from Catterick to Middlesbrough and that was when I changed from train to bus at Darlington. The bus was a single decker and a half-hourly service. I joined the wartime queue and saw I would not make the first bus. I did not make the second either, medal ribbon or not. I was put on one side by the conductress and told "workers first". The same thing happened half an hour later and again after that, and it was the fifth bus I caught. On the ride I saw the workers showing each other the brass petrol lighters they had made at work.

I had a month's leave and it's strange that I had not been missed. The locals thought I was always on leave and wanted to know how I did it when others were out fighting. Even my dog came up and wagged its tail as if I had only been out to buy a paper.

I had brought a few lemons home with me and they looked a bit dry now, but the next night at the local ARP whist drive my wife put two of them up for auction to raise funds. They fetched 19 shillings *[95 pence]*.

I spent the next seven or eight months at Catterick just passing the time away as postman and playing billiards, and was at last sent to Morpeth on the other side of Newcastle.

Morpeth was the home of a training regiment. Here one was either discharged or upgraded and sent back to duty once more. We first had to complete a physical test: running a mile in such and such a time, jumping so high and so long. I could do this but one sergeant could not do the long jump. It looked so deliberate. The two

Back to Blighty

big gym mats were pulled a yard apart and the jump was from the start of the first mat to the middle of the second. We were not in gym kit but slacks and vests. The sergeant was six feet tall and came in a stumbling run right across the first mat and just managed to clear the gap between the mats. The instructor looked at him and walked up to him.

"Sergeant, a man of your build can't do better than that?" The sergeant dropped his slacks down to his feet. One of his thighs was just bone covered with skin, the muscle had been shot off. How he had kept his leg I do not know but some doctor had performed a miracle which allowed him to walk; but jump, no. The instructor was very apologetic and contrite and would not let him continue.

As for me, nothing worried me, not even the time we went out to learn map reading from an instructor who had never been abroad. I thought of that heroic little lieutenant who had told us to be fastidiously pedantic all that time ago, and wondered how this instructor would get on in the desert with no prominent objects on which to set his map.

But there had to be something. It came with the RSM's parade for arms drill. We were 30 sergeants and upwards standing like a squad of recruits, learning how to stand to attention and to slope arms.

I thought of the times I had stood on the parade ground

in winter learning the same stuff in 1926 and 1927, of the time when I had stood so long in the frosty morning that my feet had frozen to the ground. I thought of the time after Dunkirk when I was the only man with rifle experience and had to train revolver men in its use; then when I trained the local defence volunteers. And here I was learning it again, a war later.

The RSM noticed, although I was in the rear rank. He told me to fall out and told another sergeant to take me to my hut. This man gave me two aspirins to soothe me and then took me to see the major.

By the time I got to him I was crying my eyes out.

"You will do no more drill, sergeant." And that was it.

The next day I saw a general. He gave me an option: stay in and do nothing till I had improved, or go out. He did not think I could hold a job and that was why he gave me the option. I chose to go out. The day I finished my six weeks leave happened to be 'VE' day. I had just lasted out.

Postscript

IN THE early 1950s I had recently started a business on my own. It had been a very bad year and I had failed to keep up my national insurance stamps. I could not put this right as at some time the stamps had risen in price and I did not know when or whether the Post Office still had the old ones in stock.

I decided to go to the main office for the area in Bromyard Avenue [*West London*], explain the position and write a cheque for the arrears.

The counter clerk said it was too big for him to deal with and I would have to see his chief. As I was not chained to the counter he seemed doubtful at leaving me but eventually went off to his chief's office with my papers. Some minutes later he returned to his position saying the chief would be out in a minute.

The chief came out with a broad smile on his face, his hand held out for a welcoming shake and said, "How are you Wal?" He was the lorry driving corporal who was with me when we looked in that horrible silo in Sicily [*page 191*].

J.W.H.

About the author

JOHN WALTER Harmer (known as Wally) was born on October 3rd, 1909, the second eldest child of John Harmer and Annie Twort. Annie went on to have 13 more children, five of whom died as babies or toddlers and two more as young adults, including Arthur who was killed by enemy action in 1941 (see page 6).

Wally grew up as one of ten over a secondhand furniture shop in Marylebone, London, in a condemned building with basic facilities.

There was no kitchen, just a gas stove on the landing, and the washing-up was done in a bowl on the table. Water had to be fetched from a tap outside in the yard

Wally's mother and father (left) outside their secondhand furniture shop in Marylebone in 1912. Wally is on his mother's right. At the age of three he already had three siblings – all sisters – the youngest a baby on her mother's lap (Eleanor Miranda, Julie Norton's mother).

and, if the jug needed refilling after dark, the children ventured out in twos to give each other courage. The three boys slept in one room, the seven girls in two rooms, all sharing beds.

Wally joined the army at the age of 17 just after the general strike of 1926 when there were two million unemployed. The army wage of "17 shillings and 6 pence *[88p]* a week and all found" was an offer he couldn't refuse. He served for three years in the Infantry and five years in the Royal Tank Corps.

When war began in 1939 he was still on Reserve and rejoined the Colours, serving right through till 'VE' (Victory in Europe) Day on May 8th, 1945.

After the war he bought a secondhand furniture and bric-a-brac shop in Acton, West London and ran it until he retired.

Wally wrote his memoir of his experiences of WW2 in 1975, referring to diary entries he made at the time. Not long after that his only copy of the book was mislaid. He

Wally, aged about three, with big sister Joan, a couple of years older. Their mother was to have eight more children after them (from 15 pregnancies).

Wally (second from left) is about 17 here, around the time he joined the army, in a rare photograph of all the siblings together. There is one sister missing (the third born), who was brought up by an aunt. Julie Norton's mother, fourth born, is third from left. Arthur is 5th from left.

died in 1998 believing it to be lost. The book came to light again after the death of his wife, Isabel Gibson, in 2003.

They are survived by a son and daughter, eight grandchildren and, to date, seven great grandchildren.

Acknowledgements

Jean Harrup, Wally's daughter, for preserving his manuscript, 80 A4 typed sheets, and recognising its importance as an historical record, as well as providing biographical details and supporting my endeavours.

Ivan Machin, of Wessex Archaeology who, with a passion for military history and over 20 years as a Reservist in the Territorial Army, identified the tanks and uniforms in Wally's photos.

Ian Norton, my husband, and **Andrew Norton**, my son, of Wessex Archaeology, for checking and querying the text and spotting typing errors.

And a fond acknowledgement to my Uncle Wally. I remember a man with a gruff manner and little small talk. Having read his account I now understand why.

J.N.

Also from Branchwood Publishing

Nice Nipper, by Julie Norton and the late Mira Harmer, finds mother and daughter travelling back in time together to Marylebone, London in the 1920s...
Mira was Wally's sister and her story touches upon why he joined the army just after his last sibling was born.

A cup of tea that is for ever England, by Mira Harmer, edited by Julie Norton, is a compilation of short stories about family life during the 1960s, originally published in the Daily Worker/Morning Star.

Hero chimps, by Julie Norton, presents mini biographies of some high profile chimps, including space travellers, Ham and Enos, Michael Jackson's Bubbles and Tarzan's side-kick Cheetah, showing how they were all manipulated by humans to entertain us or act as celebrity accessories.

Available from Amazon Books.

Printed in Great Britain
by Amazon